The Herb Alpert File

Stephen V. O'Rourke

© 2008 by Stephen Vincent O'Rourke
All rights reserved.

ISBN: 978-0-6151-7300-9
LCCN

Printed in the United States of America.

The Herb Alpert File

Dedicated to Herb Alpert and TJB Fans around the World

Contents

I	Young Man With A Horn	1
II	The Brass Are Coming	15
III	Going Places	23
IV	Beat of The Brass	43
V	Wade In The Water	53
VI	The House of A&M	61
VII	Keep Your Eye On Me	79
VIII	Second Wind	93

Appendixes	101
Discography	
Chronology	
Bibliography	

1

Young Man With A Horn
1957-1962

The music scene had never seen anything quite like it. Unlike Beatle mania the Tijuana Brass sound was a cross generational, multicultural phenomena. And in April of 1966 it reached its zenith: five Herb Alpert albums sat in the US Top 20 during the same week! Even the Beatles and Elvis never accomplished that feat. Herb Alpert and the Tijuana Brass could be heard everywhere in the mid-sixties: on AM radio, at pool parties, at shindigs…even at the White House and at concert halls before royalty. The road to this extraordinary success story began quietly…. in LA…in the mid 1930's….

The funny thing is, Herb Alpert never really thought of himself as a trumpet player. Long before becoming perhaps the most famous trumpet player in the world, the young Herbie Alpert found himself working anonymously, in obscurity, as a producer

The Herb Alpert File

and arranger in the smoky offices of the late 1950's Los Angeles music scene. Although he showed talent as an arranger, it was always for other artists. Herb Alpert as a pop star in the late '50's and early '60's was non-existent, and the thought of landing a Gold record with a trumpet led instrumental was preposterous to even fathom.

Born on March 31, 1935 in depression era Los Angeles, Alpert hailed from a close-nit Jewish family that had music in its roots. Herb's father Louis hailed from Kiev, Russia and although a tailor by trade, was also a talented mandolin player. Mom Tillie meanwhile had her roots in Romania and was herself taught violin at a young age. Herb's older brother David was a talented young drummer. Aside from summer vacations on Catalina Island, music was the main source of entertainment in the Alpert household.

The Alpert parents perhaps weren't too surprised then one day when they arrived home from a vacation to see a trumpet in the house. "My husband and I had gone away for the weekend to a place called Murietta Hot Springs," related Tillie Alpert, "and when we got home there was a horn in the house. We asked the children where it came from and Herb said, 'I rented it from school with my allowance,' I asked him how long he was allowed to keep it, and he said six months."

Young Man With A Horn

Eventually the young man with the horn got some serious training from local jazz trumpeter Pappy Mitchell. Mitchell, the author of several instruction books, inspired the young Herb Alpert with a philosophy that pervaded in Alpert's odyssey during the 1960's, "Life's a candy store," Mitchell declared, "You can take whatever you want from the shelf-but you have to work for it."[1]. The hard work of practicing eventually paid off and instilled a sense of dedication that Alpert would carry on into adulthood. "It became kind of a habit, like brushing my teeth, a discipline that I very much appreciate today", Alpert related in a 1966 interview[2] at the height of his fame.

Alpert did work hard, both at school and in learning to the play the trumpet in the late 1940's and early 1950's while attending Fairfax High School in Los Angeles. He briefly entertained the idea of being a classical horn player and was brought under the wing of San Francisco Symphony first trumpeter Ben Klazkin. Klazkin loved the sound of the young Alpert's horn exclaiming, "God I love the way you play!" when hearing the 13 year old play in 1948. Eventually however Alpert was pulled into the realm of pop music, first with the swing jazz

---

[1] '*The Adroit Muse, The Artful Merchant and the Appetite for Music*' by Timothy White contained on the webpage-'Herb Alpert, Jerry Moss and the History of A&M Records" accessed on http://members,aol.com/josonmus/Amhistory.html

[2] Current Biography 1967

The Herb Alpert File

of Harry James and then by a particular hit by Ray Anthony.

A veteran of Glenn Miller and Tommy Dorsey bands Anthony led his own band by the time he scored the 1950 hit, 'Young Man With A Horn'. Played regularly on the Los Angeles radio station KPFK, 'Young Man' turned Alpert onto record buying and the growing Los Angeles jazz scene. When not out playing with his own fledgling ensemble, The Colonial Trio, Alpert was soaking up the sounds of Chet Baker and Gerry Mulligan, two of the many class acts that had migrated west in the early 1950's.

Alpert's band was a talented group and had come to life in wake of Herb's brother David's band, which practiced regularly in the Alpert house. Herb's group eventually made it onto the local television program *High Talent Time* and after winning 8 consecutive contests became a much sought after attraction in the local restaurant club scene.

Upon high school graduation from Fairfax High in Los Angeles in 1955[3] Herb Alpert, "*Young Man-with a Horn*" enrolled at the University of Southern California, majoring in Music in 1954. His college days would be short-lived however and after a hedonistic period of, "playing every night, chasing

---

[3] Other famous Fairfax graduates include Mickey Rooney, Robert Wagner, Cyd Charisee, Gower Champion and David Janssen.

Young Man With A Horn

as many girls as I could and being a bellhop and playing on the weekends" at the Paradise Resort in Ontario, California, Alpert decided he needed to clean up his act[4]. Rather than pursue his studies at USC, Alpert voluntarily had his named moved up on the US Army draft list and entered the service at Fort Ord in Monterey in 1955.

Alpert's musical career continued while he was in the Army and he formed a marching band while in basic training. Training was a bit easier for musicians as Alpert wryly noted, "Instead of carrying M-1 rifles on our backs on these brutal runs, we carried our instruments. It was fun!"

Alpert's time in the service also exposed him to musicians from other parts of the country and made him a bit humble when it came to sizing up his own talent. "After basic training I was sent to Fort Knox, Kentucky and that's when I realized I wasn't as good a trumpet player as I thought I was. There were trumpet players from all over the country, and especially from New York, and they did things I could only think of doing. It was a nice eye-opener for me."

Another eye-opener for the young Alpert came when he was stationed at the Presidio in San

---

[4] *'The Adroit Muse, The Artful Merchant and the Appetite for Music'* part 4 by Timothy White contained on the webpage-'Herb Alpert, Jerry Moss and the History of A&M Records" accessed at http://members,aol.com/josonmus/Amhistory.html

The Herb Alpert File

Francisco. As a member of the 6th Army Band Alpert was commissioned to play at all major public functions, including parades, concerts and funerals. One particular day caused Alpert to reconsider a military life forever. On one solemn Sunday poor PFC Alpert was forced to play revelry at no less than 18 funerals. It was an experience that made a lasting impression on Alpert and drove him to make the most and get the most out of life.

Before leaving the army with an Honorable Discharge in 1956 Alpert had married his high school sweetheart, Sharon Lubin and began expanding his jazz library with works by Charlie Parker, Miles Davis and Clifford Brown. With his wife, a family would begin with the birth of a son, Dore, and a daughter Eden. With an expanding musical appetite Alpert would soon make connections in the Los Angeles music scene with influential people like Lou Adler and Sam Cooke.

Early Days: Adler, Cooke and Keen

The road that would lead to the creation of the Tijuana Brass began in 1957 when Herb Alpert met Lou Adler. Adler is one of the more interesting figures in the entertainment world and would eventually launch several of the music industries most successful independent record labels, namely Dunhill and Ode. In the late 1950's Adler, like Alpert, was still finding his way. Producer, arranger, composer, performer; all hats were tried on to see if one, or any of them fit[5].

Sometime in 1958 the duo began working with Keen Records in Los Angeles, ostensibly as music publishers. Eventually they were assigned to compose for a young, gifted, soul singer named Sam Cooke. Cooke had just scored a #1 for Keen Records with the classic *'You Send Me'* and with the help of Alpert and Adler put out another true classic in *'Wonderful World'* in 1960.

Not content to remain totally in the background, Alpert himself released two singles in1959, the now hard to find *Hully Gully* (credited to the Herbie Alpert Sextet) on Andex Records (Andex 34036) and the equally obscure *Sweet Georgia Brown* on Carol Records (Carol 700). Alpert and Adler even teamed up as *Herb B.Lou* with *The Trial* (Arch 1607) also in1959. Needless to say none of the above mentioned records made the slightest dent in the US charts.

One other short and successful alliance Alpert had with Adler during those early days was with the surf duo Jan & Dean. *Baby Talk* (Dore 522), arranged by Alpert, produced by Adler and recorded *by* Jan Dean, launched the surf duo's career *by* hitting the

---

[5] Alpert even did a one-off acting job, appearing in the DeMille epic, The Ten Commandments, in a very minor role. Also in 1957-58 Alpert worked as a gym instructor near his Los Angeles home.

The Herb Alpert File

Top Ten in 1959. When Jan & Dean migrated to Liberty Records in 1960 the Alpert/Adler alliance came to an effective end.[6]

Alpert returned to singing and arranging in 1961 and through a deal with RCA Victor issued two singles that year. Both were issued under the name of *Dore* Alpert and both were miserable failures. The record buying public was not quite ready for a vocalist named Alpert.[7]

A&M, as in Alpert and Moss

Jerry Moss was a bright young Jewish music industry executive from the Bronx. With a small amount of money and a lot of enthusiasm he headed west to Los Angeles as the 1960's dawned. Already and adept promotion man Moss hoped to expand his area of expertise to include music publishing and record producing.

Sometime in 1961 Moss ran into Herb Alpert at a bar near Liberty Records, where Alpert had been recording. Despite his failures at RCA Victor Alpert was still pursuing a career as a vocalist and was working on a new song called, *'Tell It To The Birds'*. Moss in turn was in need of some horn ar-

---

[6] One other Top 20 hit for Alpert & Adler came in 1960 with 'Alley Oop' as performed by Dante & the Evergreens.

[7] Rumours regarding the Dore Alpert recordings include- that Dave Alpert, Herb's brother is actually the singer on these records and not Herb.

rangements on a track he was working on called, *Love Is Back In Style*[8], so he asked Alpert if he wouldn't mind contributing some trumpet sounds to the song.

Realizing that they were both spending their own hard earned money on the two songs Moss reasoned that they could double their chances for success by pooling their resources and forming their own record company. On July 25, 1962 Carnival Records was launched with the release of the *Dore* Alpert vocal *'Tell It To The Birds'*. Although not much a commercial success, *'Tell It To The Birds'* did garner the attention of A&R man Wink Martindale who promptly bought the master tape from Alpert and Moss for $750[9]. This money was deposited right back into the bank account of Carnival Records and helped finance the production and release of the Moss produced *Love Is back In Style'*.

Unfortunately *'Style'* was not in style and disappeared without a trace- so it was back to the drawing board for Alpert and Moss. One of the first things Alpert and Moss did was to change the name of Carnival Records to A&M Records[10]. Taking the

---

[8] This song was eventually released in July 1962 on Carnival, the artist was Charlie Robinson

[9] 'Birds sold approximately 12-15,000 copies in the LA area, earning Alpert and Moss a nifty $3,500..

[10] Before it began generating royalties, A&M was simply a division of Moss' publishing company Irving Music.

The Herb Alpert File

name from the initials of the two partners' surnames. The name change had come about when another record company named Carnival Records was discovered to be still operating. In any event those few early releases by Alpert and Moss on Carnival Records are now rare collector's items and probably worth a small fortune.

A&M Records itself was originally but a division of Moss' publishing company, Irving Music, and used as a business address Alpert's garage. ""We had a desk, piano, piano stool, a couch, coffee table and two phone lines. And that for the two of us worked out very well, because we could go over the songs on the piano and make phone calls to the distributors. We also had an answering service at the time. I'd do all my own billing.[11]"

Although his career as a singer had floundered Alpert was still hesitant to begin marketing himself as an instrumental performer. "How many distinct trumpet styles have there Bix Beiderbecke, Louis Armstrong, Harry James~, Diz Gillespie, Miles Davis, Clifford Brown, the greatest of them all in my book...Harry Busse-in a different way.. I suppose. Not many. Well I wanted some identity of my own.", he quipped in an early interview.[12]

---

[11] This quote and much early history of A&M can be found at http://www.onamrecords.com/

[12] Coronet April, 1966

Young Man With A Horn

Throughout the spring of '62 however Alpert the musician began to develop despite his reservations. Work had begun on the recording of a track called *'Twinkle Star'*, written by another Alpert acquaintance Sol Lake. a bandleader. The track would evolve into *'The Lonely Bull* 'as Herb Alpert himself explained in a 1965 interview:

"For *hours* we'd been trying to find just the right sound for a tune called "*Twinkle Star*". When we started getting stale I suggested we take a break and go down to Tijuana to the bullfights. That's when it hit me! Something in the excitement of the crowd, the traditional mariachi music -the trumpet call heralding the start of the fight, the yelling, the snorting of the bulls, *it all clicked*. When we got back I rearranged "*Twinkle Star*", giving it a mariachi flavor and tempo using trumpets, piano, drums and mandolins."

Moss and Alpert both felt very good about the new recording, "But we both knew it needed another dimension," Alpert recalled, "after all you're competing with 250 other records which show up at radio stations every single week." The "other dimension" added to *'The Lonely Bull* 'came via authentic crowd noises recorded by Alpert, Moss and their engineer friend Larry Levine[13].

---

[13] Levine, a Phil Specter protégé, later headed Gold Star Studios, site of many early 'Brass sessions.

The Herb Alpert File

The remaining element to complete the song was to admonish it with a band name, the "group" at this point consisting of Alpert and several studio musicians. Despite having reservations over being labeled as a "Latin" act Alpert was satisfied with the name Jerry Moss had coined: The Tijuana Brass, realizing, "that if you can't remember a groups name, it's dead before it starts. Tijuana Brass seemed to have nice retention value."

Against the advice of record industry professionals Moss and Alpert decided to press the record themselves[14] and officially launch A&M Records in August of 1962-with themselves being the promotion staff, visiting radio stations and retailers up and down the West Coast. It was in the City by the Bay, San Francisco, where a young Alpert had been stationed as a soldier six years previous that *'The Lonely Bull'* found it's first radio audience. "One airplay in San Francisco was all it took," Alpert remembered, "the switchboard lit up and word of mouth took it from there.[15]"

Late 1962 it turned out was a perfect time to release an instrumental 45-rpm. Two major instrumental hits had in fact had just gone into the Top US 20; Stan Getz and Charlie Byrd's *Desafinado*

---

[14] Virtually all A&M records were manufactured by Monarch Record Manufacturing until 1979.

[15] Biography Annual 1967

Young Man With A Horn

(Verve 10260) and Booker T. and The MG's classic *Green Onions* (Stax 127). So with reasonably high expectations Moss and Alpert had good reason to smile when '*The Lonely Bull* '(A&M 103) entered Cashbox magazine's chart at #100 on October 20, 1962[16].

Within four weeks '*Bull* had climbed over 70 places and stood at #29. The "Tijuana" sound was catchy and fresh and instrumental hits were dominating the scene. By December when *'Telstar'* (London 9561) by the Tornadoes hit #1 'The Lonely Bull' by the virtually non-existent Tijuana Brass stood at #6 on Billboard's hit singles chart. In some regional charts 'The Lonely Bull' was even listed as the #1 single in the country.[17] After six weeks in the Top 10 'Bull had sold close to 800,000 copies[18].

As 1962 came to a close Alpert and co. had completed the first full lengthed album for A&M Records, a twelve track collection of mariachi sounding instrumentals aptly titled *The Lonely Bull* (A&M 101) It became a sizable hit on the album charts breaking into the Top 40 in January of '63. Music critic Gene

---

[16] 'Bull entered the Billboard chart one week after Cashbox, in the October 27th issue.

[17] Daily Northwestern, Oshkosh, WI 12/27/62- 'Bull is listed at #1 on the Nation's Top Ten chart

[18] With over 700,000 copies sold, 'The Lonely Bull' was awarded a Gold Disc award by the RIAA for $1,000,000 in sales.

The Herb Alpert File

Telpner wrote that *The Lonely Bull* was "an unusual album...that brings to life the noise and color, the confusion and motion of south of the border."[19]

In spite of it's popularity with the record buying public many critics saw The Tijuana Brass as purely a west coast act and thought that it would never catch on "east of Phoenix". Over the course of the years 1963 and 1964 the nay sayers appeared to be right as subsequent Tijuana Brass releases would remain south of the Top 40 border and lead Alpert and Moss to wonder about their distinct "ameriachi" sound.

But the financial success of the single *'The Lonely Bull'* had firmly established both Herb Alpert the musician and Herb Alpert the executive and in time would lead to greener pastures.

---

[19] Winnipeg Free Press 1/19/63

The Brass Are Coming
1963-1964

The years of 1963 and 1964 were years of growth for Herb Alpert and his fledgling new record company. The unexpected success of 'The Lonely Bull' would allow A&M Records to expand its roster of talent as well as its staff and Alpert's new found wealth would enabled him to live with greater comfort and raise his two children with his wife Sharon in his North Hollywood home.

In fact Alpert would remain very close to home: in the *family garage*. Like many fledgling record companies of the day, A&M Records was originally a garage operation. A&M's first employee was Jolene Burton, a former Capitol Records hand, who eventually became the account manager, after spending the early days sleeving and packing albums in Alpert's humble corporate abode. Other early A&M employees included eventual label president Gil Friesen and recording engineer Larry Levine.

The Herb Alpert File

Early Alpert associate and Dante & the Evergreens member Don Drowty remembered the time well, "Many of the best records of the day were coming out of garage operations. When I started helping Jerry and Herb pack and ship records from Herb's garage, nothing could have seemed more natural in the LA record world- or more exciting.[20]"

Absent from the hit singles chart during this two year period Alpert and Moss would never the less go forward perfecting the newly dubbed "ameriachi" sound with two new albums, *'Tijuana Brass Vo1ume 2* and *South Of The Border*. Both albums would eventually become best sellers but neither would spawn hit singles at the time of their release, leading many in the music world to realize that the Tijuana Brass sound may have been appealing to as many people *over* 30 as under. The teen market that Alpert thought would be his core audience would be a little harder to keep[21].

By March of 1963 the follow up single to 'The Lonely Bull, 'Marching Thru Madrid' (A&M 706) was issued. But much to the disappointment of Alpert and Moss the new single spent but two weeks on the chart, peaking at #90 in Cashbox magazine. Doubts began to set in among the industry as to whether The Tijuana Brass would be but one hit

---

[20] ibid

[21] 'The Lonely Bull' 45 made a profit of some $180,000 for the new record label, more than enough to sign new artists Julius Wechter, Waylon Jennings and Lucille Starr in 1963.

wonders; a novelty act from 1962, much like The Tornados, a UK band that hit #1 in late '62 with 'Telstar'.

Perhaps to hedge their bets on whether the "Tijuana Brass" would sustain it's success Alpert and Moss launched an alternative to it known as The Baja Marimba Band (A&M 104) toward the end of 1963. Led by Julius Wechter, The Baja Marimba Band would mirror the Tijuana Brass releases with a series of tongue in cheek good time albums. Wechter scored big when he wrote 'Spanish Flea' for Alpert in '66, the same year the' Marimba Band had a hit with 'Portuguese Washerwoman' and he would be a valuable fixture at many Tijuana Brass recording sessions.

Moss and Alpert took great pride in those early sessions as A&M Records transformed from an idea to a real company. Moss reminisced in an interview ten years later about recording sessions for George McCurny, "Herb was the leader and arranger and played two or three instruments. It was our first really big session, an emotional experience. Watching Herb conduct the orchestra. I thought we'd gone legit, actually conducting a string orchestra for A&M Records. We had tears in our eyes"[22].

When not working with other artists Alpert would spend much of '63 and '64 searching for material for the Tijuana Brass to "ameriachi-cize"- as well as recruit the personnel that would actually be-

---

[22] 'Two Lonely Bulls' by Judith Sims, Rolling Stone 10/12/72

The Herb Alpert File

come the 'Brass when live performances were to be given. June of 1963 saw the very first incarnation of Herb Alpert's Tijuana Brass give their first public performance, at The Crescendo in Los Angeles, but this line up was short lived[23]. Instead of continuing with live performances Alpert retired into the recording studio to complete work on 'Volume 2' (A&M 103).

This second Tijuana Brass album was issued toward the end of 1963 and despite not having a lead hit single, it would eventually make a strong showing on the U.S. album charts when the TJB craze hit home[24].

Imperfectly timed to coincide with the arrival of The Beatles the album still managed to break the Top 20 but when the new single Mexican Drummer Man (A&M 732) bombed in February 1964 it was apparent that the Tijuana sound was no match for Beatlemania- not yet anyway. Dominating both the single and album charts in a way never before seen The Beatles would begin 1964 at #1 and end 1964 at #1. Aside from the emergence of bossa nova via The Girl From Ipanema (Verve 10323) by Stan Getz

---

[23] Early Tijuana Brass members included Bob Edmonson on trombone, Julius Wechter on percussion, Bud Coleman on mandolin, Bill Riley on guitar and Mel Taylor on drums. Also playing on early TJB sessions was female bassist Carol Kaye and drum legend Hal Blaine. It is unclear who exactly played with Alpert for that first 1963 concert, besides Alpert, Edmonson and guitarist Pat Senatore.

[24] Jerry Moss estimated that in their original release the first 3 Brass albums sold a combine 60,000 copies.

and Astrid Gilberto 1964 was the year of The Beatles with little room left for *Ameriachi.*

Alpert responded to Beatlemania the only way he knew how: by making the songs of Lennon & McCartney his own. A Tijuana recording of the Beatles 'All My Loving'. along with a cover of the Louie Armstrong hit 'Hello Dolly' were recorded during his late 1964 sessions at Gold Star Studios. Also recorded was the finger snapping 'Mexican Shuffle*'* (A&M 742) which became the new Tijuana Brass single in August of '64, but like it's two predecessors failed to make the magical Top 40 plateau.

All of these new recordings would be featured on album number three *'South Of The Border'* (A&M 108), which was issued at the end of 1964. The album would get a sales boost from an unexpected source when a bubble gum company, Clark Teaberry, leased the track 'Mexican Shuffle' and featured it on a TV commercial. Young listeners scrambled to get a copy of the song, which was now only available on the album, belatedly sending the long player on to the US LP charts.

The 'Brass Takes Form

Calls for live performances were mounting, leading Alpert to finally get a permanent Tijuana Brass ensemble together. Not one of Spanish or Mexican descent the musicians who made up the TJB were as Alpert joked, "*four salamis, two bagels and an American cheese.*" Aside from front man Alpert the lineup that would remain unchanged for

The Herb Alpert File

years consisted of Lou Pagani on piano, John Pisano on guitar, Pat Senatore on bass, Bob Edmonson on trombone, Tonni Kalash on second trumpet, and drummer Nick Ceroli.

Trombonist Bob Edmonson was the only TJB member that took part in the original 1962 'Lonely Bull' session. An LA native like Alpert, Edmondson had fine credentials having played with the like of Perez Prado, Harry James and Benny Goodman among many others. Edmonson got along well with Alpert and Moss and his fine sense of humor earned him the title of Resident Comedian among Tijuana Brass members[25].

Nick Ceroli and Pat Senatore seem to have both initiated their connection to Alpert at that 1963 nightclub appearance. Ceroli, a top-notch jazz drummer had previous experience with jazz greats Stan Kenton, Ray Anthony and Les Brown before joining the 'Brass full-time. Senatore likewise had stellar jazz connections having also played with Kenton and Brown. In fact he had done a Christmas tour of Vietnam with Brown in 1965.

The Tijuana Brass' second trumpeter Tonni Kalash was a San Francisco native who had migrated south to attend college in the late 1950's. Kalash had first played with Alpert, circa 1960 at a gig at the LA City College and was added to the 'Brass lineup to specifically add "the intricate, crucial trumpet work that was to be the *TJB sound*.[26]"

---

[25] 'The Sound of the Brass', TV Week Magazine (Pasadena), 4-23-67

[26] ibid

The Brass Are Coming

Studio guitarist John Pisano was hired as a permanent member after playing at the *Whipped Cream* album sessions in late 1964. A master of the 12-string electric guitar Pisano had worked as a session player for several years in LA, cutting some fine sessions with the likes of Johnny Mathis, Tony Bennett and Peggy Lee

The final member of the 'Brass to get the call from Alpert was Pennsylvania native Lou Pagani, a talented arranger who'd paid his dues with Louis Prima, Tommy Dorsey and Ella Fitzgerald. Like Alpert, Pagani was a devout family man with a wife and two children and was hesitant to join the band when first offered in 1965 and as he noted in a 1967 interview "nobody had any idea where it was going to go"[27].

In time, thanks to a unique and ahead of its time profit-sharing arrangement, the Tijuana Brass members would become the highest paid sidemen in business. The 'Brass would initiate one of the most successful concert tours ever with a performance in Pasadena, California in May of 1965[28]. Life, Herb Alpert and The Tijuana Brass were in happy harmony and the good times were only beginning.

---

[27] ibid

[28] The TJB opened for Roger Miller at the Pasadena Civic Auditorium on May 29, 1966.

Going Places

Going Places
1965-1967

Few artists in the history of popular music have ever experienced a period of success like Herb Alpert experienced during the three-year period of 1965 through 1967. From June 1965 when *Whipped Cream & Other Delights* entered the US album charts until October 1967 when *A Banda* hit #1[29] on the US hit single list, Herb Alpert and his Tijuana Brass could do no wrong. In addition to selling millions of records during this period the 'Brass also became one of the top live attractions in the world, selling out venues from *Hollywood* to Monaco.

The Tijuana Brass' march to the top of the entertainment world was a well-calculated, step-by-step process. A series of strategic concerts, per-

---
[29] Billboard Adult Contemorary Chart

The Herb Alpert File

formed over the course of the summer of '65[30]-complimented with a few well-placed press releases-and lots of airplay on AM radio and the whole country became gripped with mariachi fever.

The release of a new single, 'Whipped Cream' (A&M 760), and it's parent album *'Whipped Cream & Other Delights'* (A&M 110) in late March of 1965 however gave little hint as to the amount of success, if any, that lay ahead. In fact the single spent only three weeks on the chart giving many the impression that the Tijuana Brass might only find success with LP sales and fail to sustain the youthful and lucrative Top 40 audience[31].

On June 12, 1965, in the wake of the TJB's first major concerts, *Whipped Cream & Other Delights* slipped into the Top 40 on Billboard magazines LP chart. This marked the beginning of one of the most successful chart runs in the history of LP's. The *Whipped Cream* long-player would chalk up 141 weeks in the Top 40 alone and remain on the outer reaches of the chart for the rest of the decade. Sporting one of the sexiest covers of all-time[32] *Whipped Cream* announced to the world that

---

[30] The TJB 1965 tour originally consisted of only 10 shows, beginning with the Memorial Day gig with Roger Miller and culminating with a Johnny Mathis gig at the Hollywood Bowl on the Labour Day Weekend in September. All of the shows were sell outs.

[31] By September the 'Whipped Cream' 45 had sold some 150,000 copies.

[32] Dolores Erickson is the model featured in a bath of shaving cream on Whipped Cream & Other Delights. She was actually three months pregnant at the time

Going Places

there was room in the Beatles-dominated pop music world for a band fun-loving, toe-tapping instrumentalists.

Aside from 'The Lonely Bull' none of the other 'Brass 45's had even broke the Top 60 so when the follow up to 'Whipped Cream', 'A Taste of Honey' (A&M 775), was issued in August to help revive sales of the album (which were themselves beginning to slip) few music scene insiders had great expectations. After four weeks *Honey* stood at only #45 on Cashbox's Hot Singles chart. But the single along with the album was about to get a second wind thanks to a series of well received live performances by the now real Tijuana Brass.

SRO-The Tijuana Brass in Concert

Seeing Herb Alpert and The TiJuana Brass perform live was more than just seeing a music concert- it was seeing polished showmanship. With the added presence of comedian Bill Dana (appearing on stage as the character "Jose Jiminez") Tijuana Brass gigs had an atmosphere of high spirits and comedic laughs all too rare in live performances. "We have to do more than just play music", bandleader and part-time comedian Herb Alpert explained, "Otherwise it's simpler to stay home and play our records."

Who made up the audience at these consistently sold out concerts was also making people take notice as the crowds consisted of as many people over fifty as there was under twenty, leaving

The Herb Alpert File

the shrewd marketeer Alpert perplexed. "I honestly thought it would be teenagers who went for the sound. But to our surprise it caught on first with adults." But the main reason diverse people liked The TJB was simple, it was happy music, signaling a celebration and as Alpert rightly noted, "People are tired of protest music and sad and angry music. We play happy music people can relate to. You don't have to be a musicologist to understand it, but it's not corny[33]."

Nothing was corny about the success of 'A Taste of Honey', during the week of November 6 it hit #6, equaling the peak position of 'The Lonely Bull' and by the month's end it had sailed all the way to #1[34], in the process becoming a Gold disc for one million copies sold. 'Honey's smashing success also helped propel *'Whipped Cream & Other Delights*' to the top of the LP chart, where it would remain for some time and eventually be certified for selling some three million copies.

The Tijuana Brass legend was solidified with a famous three-week gig in New York in October of 1965. At a time when TJB lp's were selling 50,000 copies a day Herb Alpert and his entourage set up camp at the Basin Street East in Manhattan with two opening acts: comedian George Carlin and bossa nova goddess Astrid Gilberto. Performing

---

[33] NY Times 8/18/66

[34] Cashbox and Billboard AC charts

Going Places

three shows a night to sell out crowds over a 21-day period the Tijuana Brass had definitely arrived

Total gross profit for A&M Records in 1965 was a whopping $6 million. At the end of the year despite a new release by the Beatles (*Rubber Soul),* A&M had two Gold albums sitting atop the US charts: *Whipped Cream..* and the newly signed We Five's *You Were On My Mind (*A&M 111*).*

Two new additions to the A&M staff included top-notch a&r man Tony LiPuma and legal counsel Abe Somer, who also served on the A&M Board of Directors. A&M also opened a second music-publishing firm in 1965, Almo Music- a name that would come to prominence again some thirty years later[35].

Somer was also the attorney for Brazilean artist Sergio Mendes, himself added to the A&M roster after his final Capitol release was issued in June of '65. Mendes and his band Brasil '66 would remain a core top selling act for A&M for many years and become an important part of the Herb Alpert saga both professionally and personally.

Overseas markets were also opening up for the Tijuana Brass in 1965. In the UK it would be a brand new Tijuana Brass track that would propel Herb Alpert to the top of the charts, not the US chart topper 'A Taste of Honey', which failed to even dent the UK top 100 best-seller chart. 'Spanish Flea', co-written by Baja Marimba leader Julius Wechter, was

---

[35] Almo *Records* was launched by Alpert and Moss in the 1990's in the aftermath of the sale of A&M to Polygram in 1990.

The Herb Alpert File

issued on the Stateside label (Stateside 25335) in December of '65 and began a chart run of some 20 weeks. 'Spanish Flea' would be the TJB's biggest UK hit ever and peak at #3 in January of 1966.

With A&M Records now firmly established thanks to the success of "ameriachi" Jerry Moss set about signing more new acts to the label. A Ritchie Valens protégé, Chris Montez, scored with a string of Top 40 singles in 1966, while other early A&M acts like The Sandpipers and the aforementioned We Five also notched major US Top 40 hits. Other acts signed during the late '60's included the pop maestros Boyce & Hart and the LA pop band The Merry-Go-Round.

But as 1966 dawned A&M's biggest act by far would continue to be The Tijuana Brass, or The TJB for short. Continuing to strike while the iron was hot, Alpert and the 'Brass were back in the studio completing another album by late 1965. *'Going Places'* (A&M 112) was the full lengthed album and it had been preceded by the release of a double A sided single, 'Zorba The Greek/ Tijuana Taxi' (A&M 787), both of which became Top 40 US hits in February of 1966. *Going Places* and *Whipped Cream & other Delights* would be the first two certified Gold albums in the history of A&M, for totally $1 million dollars in sales each.

Grammy's and TV Specials

Recognition for all of the past year's hard work came to Herb Alpert on March 15, 1966, barely four years since he and Jerry Moss had be-

Going Places

gun the A&M/TJB saga. Herb Alpert was a proud man being honored with three Grammy Awards at the annual ceremonies. 'A Taste of Honey' was the reason for the awards, winning for Record of the Year, Best Instrumental and Best Instrumental Arrangement. Jerry Levine, the man behind the TJB sound as Gold Star Studios, also copped a Grammy that night for Best Engineered Album for his work on *'Whipped Cream & Other Delights'*.

Just prior to the Grammy Awards Herb Alpert and his Tijuana Brass were in London performing their first concert there to a sellout crowd. The new single 'Spanish Flea' (London) had become their biggest foreign hit and the concert launched what amounted to a world tour. Headline SRO concerts soon following at Carnegie Hall in New York and The Greek in Los Angeles. After a TJB command performance at the White House Correspondents Dinner, former Postmaster General beamed, "Best live entertainment I've seen in Years"[36].

Numerous television appearances also followed allowing the 'Brass to sustain its wave of popularity at a fever pitch. Throughout 1966 and 1967 the TJB appeared on variety shows by Danny Kaye, Dean Martin and of course the veritable Sunday night program of Ed Sullivan.

In those days long before MTV, the Tijuana Brass were everywhere on the TV dial. TV critic Clay Gowran declared in his May 8, 1966 column

---
[36] 'Horns Of Plenty' Newsweek 4/25/66

The Herb Alpert File

('Bull Market for Tijuana), "Alpert and his swinging sidemen get more TV than Hubert Humphrey. In a recent week, the Tijuana Brass appeared one night on CBS-TV's Danny Kaye hour, the next on NBC's Dean Martin Show, and on the next night, the combo starred at the White House correspondents' annual dinner in Washington."[37]

In their detailed 25 minute discussion Alpert also noted to Gowran the TJB's recent UK appearances and just what the TJB sound was all about. "We did three shows on TV for the British Broadcasting Corporation and had one theater date." In describing the Tijuana Brass sound Alpert stated, "It's sort of a fusion of the mariachi sound of Mexico with a jazz undercurrent. But I haven't really thought out a description and I don't want to try for one. I have a feeling that if I analyze it, it might become a formula. And music isn't made by formula, or by an IBM machine, it comes from the body and the mind."

With a well-calculated marketing campaign A&M Records was able to capitalize on the Tijuana craze by re-issuing all of the 'Brass' previous albums in the spring of 1966. By May 1st all of the TJB titles were on the bestseller list-in a seen reminiscent of Beatlemania two years previous. Hollywood columnist Mary Campbell declared in her Associated Press syndicated column that Herb Alpert and the TJB's music was "buoyant, pungent,

---

[37] The Abilene Reporter-News 5/8/66

polished" and "by far the hottest sound on record today."[38]

A&M Buys the Lil Tramps Home

In the summer of '66 A&M Records announced the purchase of an old movie studio once owned by the great Charlie Chaplin, from Columbia Broadcasting Systems (CBS) fueling rumors that the "unselfconsciously handsome[39]" Alpert would venture into acting. By April of '67 the rumors were somewhat confirmed with the presentation of the CBS-TV "Herb Alpert Variety Hour" program. But Alpert tred slowly in the path toward the silver screen and never fully committed to any major film project.

Many were keen for the 'Brass to do a full-fledged movie, a 'la *Hard Days Night*, and producer Bill Perlberg even thought that he had a done deal with the band to do such an undertaking. Perlberg, one-time manager to Al Jolson, felt that the TJB were "the top show business act today" and told columnist Leonard Lyuns in November of 1966 that he had a deal to produce "the Herb Alpert Movie"[40].

Perhaps the closest the Tijuana Brass maid it to the silver screen however was when NBC's top-rated comedy *Get Smart* spoofed Alpert and the 'Brass in an episode that saw Agent 86 (played by

---

[38] Platter Parade The Daily Review 5/1/66, Hayward, CA

[39] Annual Biography 1967

[40] Leonard Lyons 11/8/66

The Herb Alpert File

Don Adams-a good friend of Bill "Jose Jimenez" Dana) infiltrated the KAOS controlled band The Tijuana Tin which was led of course by the trumpeter Herb Talbert.

Purchasing the Charlie Chaplin Studios at 1416 North La Brea Avenue in Hollywood marked a formal and literal solidification of the A&M corporation, which now employed some 32 individuals. Jolene Burton accompanied Jerry Moss for the meeting that closed the real estate purchase and literally put A&M Records on the map. " "With absolutely no idea that we would possibly, conceivably buy it, Jerry and I went over with the real estate people and the attorney. Herb was out of town. When we drove through the gates, I took one look at Jerry and said, 'We just bought ourselves a piece of property!' Immediate enthrallment. When Herb came back he took one look at the place and had exactly the same feeling that Jerry did. There was something about going through those gates that felt like home.[41]" Helping make the Chaplin studios a real home for the A&M family was David Alpert, Herb's older brother, who oversaw the conversion of the sprawling film studio into executive offices and recording studios. The North La Brea site would serve as the A&M home for over three decades before finally being abandoned in 1999 by Universal Music Group.

---

[41] http://www.onamrecords.com/

Going Places

The album *'Going Places'* meanwhile was doing just that- spending six weeks at #1 on the US charts and along with all previous TJB albums would be certified as Gold Discs by the Recording Industry of America at a ceremony in Hollywood.

A second double A sided single (meaning that both sides of the record would be considered as separate entries on the chart) was issued in April of 1966 with 'Spanish Flea' being coupled with 'What Now My Love' (A&M 792). Both would be Top 40 hits, giving the Tijuana Brass five Top 40 hits since Whipped Cream had reached only #68 a year earlier.

A Golden Avalanche

Sales figures would now go through the roof, with the release of the complete LP of *'What Now My Love'* (A&M 114) in May 1966. With *'What Now My Love'* following it's two predecessors to the top of the lp chart and the entire 'Brass catalogue now re-entering the list a unique situation occurred that saw Herb Alpert and The Tijuana Brass place five albums in the Top 20 in the same week, four of which were also in the Top 10. No other recording artists, the Beatles and Elvis included, have ever accomplished such an amazing feat.

So stunning was the 'Brass success at this time that music critic Bob Considine articulated that, "There hasn't been anything as spectacular as the

The Herb Alpert File

rise of Alpert's band in the memory of the grayest beard in the music business"[42].

Columnist Hal Boyle in fact saw Alpert as the slayer of rock 'n roll itself in his article 'Herb Alpert broke the Sound-Barrier to the Tune of $-Millions'[43], "The sound-barrier they broke was the sound of rock 'n roll which has dominated the music world for years. They created a rollicking new sound, a sound in which Alpert wedded Dixieland jazz and spirited rhythms of Mexico's strolling mariachi bands." Boyle also noted Alpert's resemblance to Rudolph Valentino with his "dark sideburns and matador build" and felt that he was truly "riding a golden avalanche" with an estimated gross of some $32 million for the year.

The large profits of 1966 led to an expansion of operations at A&M Records and its affiliated companies. New executives in 1966 included Bob Fead (distribution), Don Graham (promotion), Dave Hubert (international publishing) and Chuck Kaye, who was installed as head of Almo and Irving Music. In total A&M placed 15 45-rpm singles and 8 long-playing albums on the US charts in 1966. The Tijuana Brass sold some 13.7 million albums for the year and unheard of amount for the time.

A large portion of the "golden avalanche" stemmed from the bright reception received for the sparkling LP *What Now My Love*. For nine weeks

---

[42] 'Herb Alpert Is Very New On the Celebrity Scene' by Bob Considine 8/30/66

[43] Idaho State Journal 8/18/66

Going Places

What Now My Love stayed at #1 on Billboard magazine's chart in the U.S. While across the Atlantic in the U.K. sales were also taking off as the three most recent albums had all gone into the British Top 20, the *'Whipped Cream'* lp reaching as high as #2.

Other foreign markets were also opening up, most notably Europe, Mexico and Australia. And soon thanks to another Alpert production South America would also be conquered.

Brasil '66 Arrives

With the profits to the A&M coffers continuing to grow Jerry Moss was able to pursue some name acts for the A&M roster and in early 1966 made a major coup when he was able sign one of Brazil's top performers Sergio Mendes to a deal. With Alpert himself overseeing the production of Mendes' first A&M disc and a shrewd selection of bossa nova hits to cover chosen, the recording sessions were a joy. Mendes' back up group, the newly renamed Brasil '66, included two female vocalists, one being the future Mrs. Herb Alpert- Lani Hall. Songs covered on the album included 'o Pato' and 'One Note Samba' as well as an inspired version of The Beatles 'Day Tripper', which became the group's first hit.

The signing of Mendes would be the first of many jazz oriented artists to A&M Records, later additions to the jazz family included Quincy Jones, Hugh Masekela and bossa nova giant Antonio Carlos Carlos Jobim. By 1969 A&M would even join in a partnership with the great jazz producer Creed Taylor and distribute his legendary CTI label for several years.

The Herb Alpert File

Presidents and Princesses

Presidents and Princesses rounded out the summer of 1966 for Herb Alpert. At the invitation of President Lyndon Johnson Alpert and his entourage played the White House on August 18 1966. One month later on September 18 royalty called as the European tour culminated with a performance before Princess Grace and her family in Monaco[44]. From Washington to the Riviera no place was out of place for "Ameriachi" it seemed.

Some critics however thought the mariachi label as inappropriate. John S. Wilson of The New York Times thought the group's instrumentation was "more twangy and thumpy than brassy. Others were not impressed at all; the San Francisco Chronicle's Ralph Gleason calling the Tijuana Brass, "a corny Latin American minstrel show", while Newsweek tried to pigeon-hole them as "the middle age answer to rock n' roll." Perhaps somewhat annoyed at the criticism Alpert told the New York Times, "I don't really know what the sound of the group is...and I don't want to know"[45].

Regardless of what label the critics put on the Tijuana Brass' music the record buying public continued to have a good time purchasing their records.

---

[44] Alpert in fact had been invited by Princess Grace herself in a letter she had sen to him to ward off the imitators. Press-Telegram, Long Beach CA 10/29/66

[45] NY Times 8/18/66

Going Places

The appropriately titled 'The Work Song' (A&M 805) became the band's next hit single (as well as the band's first video, shot at the old Chaplin soundstage) hitting #18 in August.

Alpert was proud of 'The Work Song' and saw it as a continuation of his quest to improve and diversify the TJB sound. "'The Work Song' is actually a jazz tune", Alpert elaborated to music critic Bob Thomas, "it was written by the brother of Cannonball Adderly. Jazz is such a rich vein of musical expression that it should be put into form that is appreciated by the entire public, not just the jazz fancier"[46].

'The Work Song' was followed on the charts towards the end of the year by Flamingo (A&M 113) and Mame (A&M 823), which both broke the US Top 30. All of these tracks were included on the twelve song LP, *S.R.O* (A&M 119), another Gold album that peaked at #2 on the US charts, being held off from #1 by new albums from The Beatles and The Monkees. The Beatles and The Monkees aside, at the close of 1966 Herb Alpert and The Tijuana Brass were the top grossing musical act in the world as each of Alpert's sidemen stood to make close to $100,000 each from their live performances alone.

The Royale Treatment

---

[46] 'The Brass Glitters' by Bob Thomas Oakland Tribune 6/20/66

The Herb Alpert File

The early part of 1967 saw the group take a brief hiatus from touring to concentrate on the recording of yet another album. These recording sessions also covered new material for the soundtrack to an upcoming James Bond spoof, Casino Royale. By April both projects were complete and on the charts. *Casino Royale* (A&M 850), a Burt Bacharach composed track, hit#27 on both the US and UK charts[47] while the new full lengthed TJB album *Sounds Like* (A&M 4124) sizzled up the lp charts with help from' Herb's hip arrangement of 'Wade In The Water (A&M 840).

Sounds Like' was another instant smash climbing to #1 within weeks of it's release and staying there for six weeks. Total sales figures for Tijuana Brass records over the past three years were close to an incredible ten million copies sold in both monophonic and stereophonic versions.

Another festive year of touring, TV appearances and awards made up the TJB agenda for 1967. On April 24th '*The Herb Alpert & The Tijuana Brass*' TV special aired on the CBS network to high ratings. Alpert spent a small fortune on this special- filming some 34 hours of song clips over a two and a half week period- at various locales like Disneyland and the LA Coliseum. Earlier in 1967, at the Grammy Awards, Alpert had walked away with two more awards, both for the single 'What Now My

---

[47] Casino Royale, also hit #1 on Billboard's AC chart for six weeks.

Going Places

Love' (winning for Best Instrumental and Best Instrumental Arrangement).

Just prior to the airing of the CBS-TV special Alpert and his band were off to the Far East and a four-day junket to Japan. Playing to a sold out crowd at the Kosei Nenkin Hall, Alpert quipped at a pre-gig press conference, "We've been on the road for three weeks and we just haven't been to the barbershop." after being asked about the TJB's long sideburns and bushy mustaches[48].

Back in Hollywood the A&M Records facilities were making the transition from a silent film back lot to a high tech recording studio and office complex. Jolene Burton and her accounts department was transformed by the installation of state-of-the-art computers and she was given the new title of Controller- becoming A&M Records first woman executive. Recording engineer Howard Holzer worked closely with Herb Alpert and Larry Levine in setting up the original A&M recording studios on one of the two soundstages once used by Charlie Chaplin and other legends of the silver screen.

With Satchmo and…LBJ

In September a dazzling variety show, showcased the TJB with comedian Jackie Vernon and jazz legend Louis Armstrong. *"And all That Brass'* featured the 'Brass playing with Armstrong on 'Mack The Knife' and other classics, as well as a poignant conversation between Alpert and Satchmo, as he

---

[48] Pacific Stars and Stripes 4-15-67

The Herb Alpert File

recounted his career and early days in New Orleans.

By October, #1 fan President Lyndon Johnson even called the' Brass back to the White House for an encore performance. In what UPI reporter Merriman Smith declared, "may be the squarest gig Alpert & Co ever encountered", the White House announced that the Tijuana Brass would be on hand for "an exciting evening of dancing in the East Room[49]". Later the gig took on an added dimension of significance that did make the evening quite exciting for Alpert and Co. when it was announced that the President of Mexico would be the guest of honor that very night. A famous picture of both presidents, beaming alongside the entire TJB, was taken and released to newspapers- showing just how un-sqare Alpert and the boys could be.

Alpert himself closed out 1967 doing what he now loved even more than performing for Presidents, Princesses and his millions of fans: mixing and recording a new album. Ensconced at Gold Star Recording Studios[50] with engineer Larry Levine, Alpert polished off the meticulous TJB set, *Herb Alpert's 9th* for autumn 1967 release.

The A&M roster continued to expand in 1967 with the signing of several legendary musicians and composers like Phil Ochs, Burt Bacharach and Wes Montgomery. Jerry Moss made a determined effort

---

[49] Brownsville Herald 10-18-67

[50] The A&M Recording studios would not open until August of 1968.

Going Places

to bring A&M into the rock scene by bringing brit stars Joe Cocker and Procul Harum into the A&M family. A&M was even able to hire ex-Beatle press agent Derek Taylor as a PR man as the Summer of Love came to a close.

On December 12 the entire A&M clan took over the top-rated ABC-TV variety show The Hollywood Palace in a show hosted by Herb Alpert and the Tijuana Brass. Giving historical performances that night on network TV in addition to Alpert and his merry sidemen was: the Baja Marimba Band, Sergio Mendes and Brasil '66, Liza Minelli, Burt Bacharach, Boyce and Hart and the great jazz guitarist -Wes Montgomery.

While it may have now seemed for many that there were few additional plateaus for Herb Alpert to reach in his career-the year of 1968 would provide a different beat to the Tijuana Brass sound and propel him to even higher levels of superstardom.

.

Beat of the Brass
1968

The year 1968 gave the world some of the best pop music ever made. It was the year of 'Hey Jude', 'Mrs. Robinson' and 'I Heard It Through The Grapevine'. And for A&M Records it was to be a year of Love in both song and spirit.

The year began much like the previous three had for the TJB with an album near the top of the LP charts. *Herb Alpert's 9th* (A&M 4134) would quickly become the band's 9th Gold album and peak at #4 on Billboard magazine's best seller list in January of 1968. One of the highlights on *9th* was Alpert's brilliant interpretation of Chico Baurque De Hollanda's 'A Banda'- originally written as a Brazilian protest song.

Newer material was soon to take up much of Herb Alpert's attention as he began working with composer Burt Bacharach on a regular basis, a collaboration that would lead to the composition of one

The Herb Alpert File

of the biggest hits of both of their careers. Bacharach's now hard to find A&M debut *Reach Out* (A&M 4131) was one of a slew of A&M releases catering to the newly named "Adult Contemporary" (or "Easy Listening") audience, an audience that in many ways was already being served admirably by Brasil '66.

Brasil '66's third album, *Look Around* (A&M 4137), took off sales wise when their version of 'The Look of Love' (A&M 924), one of many, became a big hit single in May. Brasil '66's 'Look climbed all the way to #4 on Billboard's Top 40 chart but had to fight off four other versions of the song: one by Dusty Springfield, one by Liza Minnelli, a~ by Burt Bacharach himself and one by yet~ A&M artist, Claudine Longet on her Look of Love album (A&M 4129). 'The Look of Love' performed by Dusty Springfield was featured in the recently completed comedic James Bond flick Casino Royale (Colgems 5005) (which featured the Tijuana Brass on the title track.

One of the reasons Alpert was working so closing with Burt Bacharach was that he had been signed on by CBS-TV to host another variety show in April and he wanted to perform some new "special" material on it. Bacharach and his songwriting partner Hal David served up Alpert a song entitled 'This Guy's In Love With You', a very un-Tijuana Brass soft sounding song that it was to return Alpert to the vocal stage for the first time in six years.

Beat Of The Brass

The Beat of the Brass-In Color!

Alpert's 1968 TV special was big news even before it aired. 'Million Dollars A Day-Tijuana Brass TV Special Is Planned for April 22' declared one headline[51]- noting the huge expense of filming the Brass in diverse locations. From a private shoot on Ellis Island to a Mardi Gras time shoot in New Orleans- Alpert's TV shows had now turned into huge extravaganzas. The Bacharach-David composition was also big news with one article declaring that it was written about "A love affair that has been the quiet inspiration behind one of the most phenomenal success stories in show business"[52]."

The Ellis Island filming came under close scrutiny and made for a humorous and poignant article by NEA Entertainment Editor Joan Crosby. In her 'Son of an Immigrant- Herb Alpert Rocks Ellis Island with His Brass.." Alpert recounted his father's arrival in America and noted whimsically that his father was now retired "and listening to the radio" in California. The article also noted that it was costing the production company some $20,000 per day to film on Ellis Island, which was closed as an immigration center in 1954.

---

[51] By Rokara Legendre (NANA)

[52] 'Sharon Is Womand Behind Alpert Notes'- The Lima News (AZ 4-21-68

The Herb Alpert File

When the program finally aired in late April it got very high ratings much like the previous year's specials[53] and immediately led to a public demand for the new vocal Tijuana Brass song, which ended the program. By May 11th a studio version had been mixed by Alpert and engineer Jerry Levine and debuted on Cashbox Magazine's chart at #84. In a mere three weeks it was already at #12 and two weeks later, on June 15th it was #2, being held off the top spot by Simon & Garfunkel and their classic Mrs. Robinson (Columbia 44511).

But a week later 'This Guy's In Love With You' (A&M 929) was the top selling record in America. It would remain at #1 for four weeks and become Herb Alpert's biggest hit single to date, eventually being certified Gold by the Recording Industry Association of America for 1,000,000 copies sold.

By July a new album was complete, *'The Beat of The Brass'* (A&M 4146) a colorful, classy package with a gatefold sleeve that featured a new stereo mix of the hit single plus ten other tracks. '*Beat* too would become a million seller and would hit #1 on the LP charts on July 6th. As of July 1968 Herb Alpert was the top selling artist in the U.S. and arguably in the world.

---

[53] Alpert's 1967 CBS special was in fact the highest rated network broadcast for the entire year.

Beat Of The Brass

A major feature article in the Los Angeles Times[54] by the great jazz critic Leonard Feather provides a unique snapshot on Alpert-mania in the summer of '68. Feather begins with a detailed description of the Alpert success story: "What do you give a fellow who has offices on three acres in Hollywood that once constituted Charlie Chaplin's residence; a new half million dollar recording studio; nine albums on the best seller lists simultaneously (three of which have been there every week for over three years); a Spanish building in which computers help estimate his fortune. What in life can there be that a trumpeter-tycoon has never had before?....Possibly a hit record as a singer."

Feather further illuminates on Alpert's appearance upon meeting him at his offices, in that Mod Squad era: "I found Alpert the other day in his cluttered, comfortable office, between editing sessions. He was neatly turned out in the conventional attire of the thoughtful and with-it young Hollywood male (yellow turtleneck, beads with peace symbol, etc)."

Feather's probing into the emergence of Alpert's vocal hit gets a detailed answer. "We were fishing around for something different to do on our television special and I asked Burt Bacharach if he would have time to write a song for me. Burt Bacharach is the greatest songwriter in the world

---

[54] ''Millionaire Herb Alpert on Top as Singer' by Leonard Feather Los Angeles Time 8-1-68

The Herb Alpert File

today. A couple of weeks later he sat down at the piano and sang *'This Guy's in Love With You'*. I flipped out. I said this would be a hit if my mother sang it!"

The article goes on to a detail discussion on potential films and TV specials and ends with Feather continuing to turn the screw on the mild-mannered Alpert. "Unflappable Alpert means what he says. At present it would seem nothing could ruffle his patience- except perhaps, the reissue of those *Dore Alpert sides*".

The Look $ of Love $

But if anything, 1968 was less about the Alpert's past than it was about looking toward the future. As it turned out 1968 would also prove to be a banner year for Sergio Mendes and his Brasil '66. The super popular pop-vocal act, produced by Alpert himself, would cap off the year with two more Top 20 hit singles (Fool On The Hill #6 and Scarborough Fair #16) plus another Gold album. These hits would turn Mendes and his lead vocalist, Lani Hall, into pop superstars and ensure that A&M continued to have a solid base as the decade came to a close.

With their coffers filling with record-breaking profits A&M Records, under the direction of Gil Frisen, could now head in directions never charted by the label before. Prolific jazz people like Wes

Beat Of The Brass

Montgomery, Antonio Carlos Jobim and Quincy Jones were soon signed by A&M, as were popular rock acts like Procul Harum and Joe Cocker. Each of these artists, but particularly Joe Cocker would contribute in the transition A&M would make over the next few years from being just another independent record label into being THE independent label. By the early 1970's A&M Records would be recognized as a musician's record company, regardless of genre or musical style.

As '68 came to a close however Herb Alpert and the TJB would still be the label's driving force notching up two more hit singles and yet another Top 40 album. A second vocal, 'To Wait For Love' (A&M 964), was the follow up to 'This Guy and was a moderate seller hitting #39 in Cashbox, #50 in Billboard.

In December the instrumental 'My Favorite Things' (A&M 1001) hit #35 on the Billboard Top 40. Taken from the seasonal classic *The Christmas Album* (A&M 3113) .My Favorite Things' and its supporting tracks, presented listeners with one of the hipper sounding Christmas sets around. Alpert was overjoyed with the '*Christmas* sessions and elaborated to Associated Press writer Mary Campbell, "We've got a 16-piece chorus, the first time we've used professional voices. There are pop tunes, with only one religious, 'Jesu, Joy of Man's Desiring'. We've got several that should transcend the two weeks that radio stations play Christmas

The Herb Alpert File

carols."[55] *The Christmas Album* would be re-issued on a regular basis over the years and would be a best-seller almost every year on the seasonal sales charts.

The year 1968 was a mere six years since 'The Lonely Bull' had propelled Herb Alpert into the American consciousness. It had been only a little over three years since the "Ameriachi" craze had taken over the US charts and TV specials.

Herb Alpert, the mild mannered man with a horn now stood as perhaps the world's top musical persona. He had mastered pop music in both instrumental and vocal forms. Elevated the concert tour to an exciting, moneymaking experience. He had bridged the generation gap by combining hipness with sentiment. And he had overseen the creation of one of the music industry's most important record companies. As he put it himself many years later, "I had reached the top of the mountain…and it was time to jump off.[56]"

---

[55] 'Alpert's Singing Liked Best' by Mary Campbell AP syndicated column

[56] Rolling Stone 12/13/79

Beat Of The Brass

Wade In the Water
1969-1970

The 1960's closed on a quiet note for the Tijuana Brass. Live appearances were reduced to a minimum and then to none at all as front man Alpert began concentrating on the growing operations of A&M Records. After seven years of center stage success it was time to bow out with the grace and class that had distinguished him from the rest of the crowd.

Single and album releases and concert performances would continue, but with sales figures far below the Alpert norm. After his first vocal hit the year before it was decided to continue in that style in 1969 as Alpert re-worked Harry Nilsson's 'Without Her' *(A&M-1015)* in April. Although a Top 40 hit (#38 on Cashbox) it was obvious that the mood of the record buying public was up for diversity in 1969.

Hard rock (Led Zeppelin) and jazzy pop (Blood, Sweat & Tears) were replacing the mellow

The Herb Alpert File

take it easy sound of The Tijuana Brass. Reflecting on his "middle of the road" image Alpert would comment years later, "I got caught in a role that was exciting at first, but it got to be dull." In spite of the public's shift in musical interests Alpert would remain popular over the next two years with two more albums in the Top 40 and another top-rated network TV special.

Alpert would close out the decade with one more Gold album, his 11th, as *Warm* (A&M 4179) broke Billboard's Top 40 in September of '69. This remarkable sales feat placed Alpert behind only Elvis and The Beatles in the Gold Record category for the decade of the 1960's.

Critics were generally kind when reviewing *Warm*- William D. Laffler felt that the album contained "a good number of surprises" and that Alpert was, "one of the most unusual musicians of the space age" having "introduced Tijuana Brass band music at a time when rock groups were the *in* people". Laffler also believed that *Warm* showed that Alpert had "lost none of his brilliance in sound"[57]. Mary Campbell felt that with *Warm* the Tijuana Brass "have changed their image" and found Alpert's voice "ingratiating"[58]. Music critic Jeff Duffield

---

[57] 'Warm by Tijuana Brass Is Must For Alpert Fans' by William D. Laffler The Coshocton Tribune 8/20/69

[58] 'Summer Brings Cloudburst of New Records' by Mary Campbell AP News features 7/26/69

Wade In The Water

was ecstatic with *Warm* and felt that "Herb Alpert shows that the magic is still there"[59]. Good reviews aside *Warm's,* failure to reach the top of the charts indicated that the Tijuana Brass had finally reached saturation point.

The Brass Are Going

As such, the winning streak of Gold records would finally come to an end with the release of *The Brass Are Coming* (A&M 4228) in late 1969 as it failed to reach Gold status despite hitting #30 and being the spin off from a TV variety special. The downward spiral would be rectified however with the issue of Herb Alpert and The Tijuana Brass' Greatest Hits (A&M 4245), became one of A&M's best sellers in the early1970's as fans clamored to get an album with all "the good stuff" on one record.

After a troublesome world tour in late 1969 and a lukewarm response to 'The Brass Are Coming', Alpert began pondering what life without the TJB would be like. Add to this the fact that his eleven year marriage[60] was also coming to an end and anyone could see that Herb Alpert needed a break.

---

[59] 'Herb Alpert Shows Magic Still There' by Jeff Duffield San Antonio Express/News 7/13/69

[60] Alpet and his first wife Sharon were divorced in 1971 after a long separation.

The Herb Alpert File

'*End of Herb Alpert and the Tijuana Brass*' screamed newspapers on Monday January 26, 1970[61] as Alpert announced he was breaking up the band. Columnist Marilyn Beck glumly noted, "It seems certain that there will be no more TJB specials with the old familiar group...and I'm told there will be no more road appearances. The Tijuana Brass are Dead. A golden era in music has ended." Although Alpert tried to retreat from the idea that the TJB was no more a few weeks later ("We're not disbanding-we're just on a temporary recess.")[62] The truth was the era of the happy sounds of the Tijuana Brass was indeed over.

Alpert's progression toward's a life after the 'Brass seemed to stall as he was attempting to find a solid vocal follow-up to 'This Guy's In Love With You' during 1970 recording sessions. After confidently recording a new Bacharach and David song entitled 'Close To You', Alpert was deflated when trusted engineer Larry Levine gave it a thumb's down. Alpert didn't issue his version of the song at the time, and as he said in the liner notes to the *Lost Treasures* cd, "I lost confidence in my singing voice and gave the song to Richard and Karen Car-

---

[61] The Daily Gleaner 1/26/70

[62] 'Herb Alpert, Brass Take Break To Watch Hair Grow' (Associated Press) 2/22/70

Wade In The Water

penter...Lucky for them and lucky for A&M Records."[63]

It would be the young brother/sister duo from southern California, The Carpenters, who would provide Alpert with a comfortable life after the demise of the Tijuana Brass. The Carpenters would be A&M Records biggest act in the early 1970's. Richard and Karen Carpenter, winners of a talent contest at the Hollywood Bowl, had submitted demo tapes to A&M that eventually found their way to label prez Alpert. Showing a good ear for talent Alpert signed them to the label in late 1969 and by the spring of 1970 they were on the charts with a reworking of 'Close To You' (A&M 1183).

Starting with that hit the duo would dominate the singles chart for the next five years. They would incredibly rack up fourteen consecutive Top 10 hits, virtually all of them being million sellers. In total The Carpenters scored a total of twenty Top 40 hits during their career easily making them the top A&M singles act ever.

Two other significant A&M acts during this period include the artsy Procul Harum and bluesy Englishman Joe Cocker. Procul Harum put out a series of well-received albums after being signed to A&M by Jerry Moss in the late 1960's; one of their best albums was the Live In Concert, which fea-

---

[63] 'Lost Treasures' liner note Shout Factory 32867 (2005)

The Herb Alpert File

tured the classic single Conquistador (A&M 1347). Joe Cocker meanwhile made a name for himself with his own unique cover versions of other people's hits; scoring in 1969 with Traffic's Feelin' Alright (A&M 1063) and in 1970 with The Beatles She Came In Through The Bathroom Window (A&M 1147).

Cocker was in fact the biggest rock act on A&M at the time with three Gold albums and a film, *Mad Dogs and Englishmen* and he was as Jerry Moss put it, "Our transitional artist.[64]" A&M PR man Bob Garcia elaborated, "Cocker opened the door. He was the greatest PR man for rock& roll to this company; he was the most honest representation of what it was about then. We grew up on Joe."

A&M Records continued to expand operations in 1969 as it positioned itself to become the leading independent record company in the world. A&M Records *Limited* was incorporated in the UK in 1969 thus alleviating the need to secure licensing deals with local UK companies. From 1963 to 1965 A&M Records were issued on Stateside in the UK and from 1965 to 1969 Pye Records issued A&M's UK product. Over the course of it's 29 year existence A&M Records Ltd overcame several controversial episodes[65]- including the infamous signing of the

---

[64] 'Two Lonely Bulls and How They Grew'-Rolling Stone 10/12/72

[65] Right off the bat it created controversy with its' first release, *A Witch is Born* by Alex Sanders. This obscure release was the actual recording of a witch's initiation into a coven!

Wade In The Water

Sex Pistols in 1977 to become a valued UK label in its' own right.

Although now somewhat of a minor act on his own label Herb Alpert would chart one last time with the Tijuana Brass in October 1970 with the beautiful and haunting 'Jerusalem' (A&M 1225), a minor hit that reached #74 on the Cashbox chart. The heyday of the 'Brass like all good things was corning to an end, a new decade with new groups and styles was emerging and A&M Records was in a perfect position to be in the forefront as the decade progressed.

The House of A&M
1971-1978

Throughout the decade of the 1970's Herb Alpert the musician evolved into Herb Alpert the executive. From his perch atop the house of A&M Alpert resided over a series of signings of significant acts who were destined to create some of the most enjoyable music of the decade. Virtually every act signed in the 1970's had a hit. From Cat Stevens to Rita Coolidge and from Billy Preston to The Police A&M Records was graced with first rate performances and top selling hits.

As the Tijuana Brass faded into retirement in 1971, British born folk singer Cat Stevens (born Stephen Georgiou) picked up the Top 40 mantle with a string of top notch singles and albums until his abrupt retirement in 1978. Beginning with the March 1971 hit 'Wild World' (A&M 1231) Stevens placed eight singles in US Top 40 over a brief three and a half *year* period. His August 1974hit was a cool horn driven cover of Sam Cooke's 'Another

The Herb Alpert File

Saturday Night (A&M 1602), a sort of dedication to the late singer by A&M Records on the 10th anniversary of his death.

Cat Stevens steamrolled on through the mid-70's with a series of well received albums but he was unable to reconcile his religious aspirations with the fast paced record industry he was surrounded by. It was visiting Jerry Moss' California home that Stevens had a revelation that he should devote himself to religion. While caught in the undertow while swimming in the Pacific Ocean, Stevens feared for his life- in a cry for help he called out to God and vowed to give it all up if he survived.

In 1978 at the height of his popularity Stevens converted to Islam and changed his name to Yusef Islam and vanished from the rock world permanently. A major loss artistically and commercially to the A&M family.

Herb Alpert's lack of chart success in 1971 seemed to confirm his reasons for closing down the original ensemble. Two singles were issued in 1971 by "Herb Alpert and the Tijuana Brass" but neither even dented the Top 100. Likewise- the reasonably received LP *Summertime* (A&M 4314) failed to have any impact in pop music or jazz circles. Three short years after *Beat of the Brass* and Herb Alpert was again south of the border when it came to having a hit record.

The House of A&M

1971's biggest A&M moneymaker,' was by far *Tapestry* (Ode) *by* Carol King. This classic album sold a then record 5.5 million copies for Ode Records, a licensing partner with A&M Records that was headed by Herb Alpert's old pal Lou Adler. *Tapestry* spawned four hit singles and played a major part in ensuring that 1971 would be A&M's most profitable year yet. At the years end the coffers showed a net profit of $32 million and as Rolling Stone magazine put it "What's good for Ode is good for A&M"[66].

Keyboardist Billy Preston was an early '70's success story for A&M after being signed in 1971. The former Beatles and Stones sideman put out a series of funky pop records that would cross over onto the singles charts. In fact beginning with the instrumental 'Outa-Space' (A&M 1320) which was certified Gold in 1972 Preston registered Gold with 'Will It Go Round In Circles' (A&M 1411) and 'Space Race (A&M1463) in 1973. A year later. Preston would round out his string of hits with the #1 smash 'Nothing from Nothing' (A&M 1544) in August 1974.

English acts would continue to weave a web of success for A&M throughout the early and mid-1970's. Beginning in 1970 Humble Pie, a bluesy hard rock quartet, started putting out long playing records that found a niche among the ever-growing "counter-culture" record buying public. 1971's *Per-*

---

[66] ibid

The Herb Alpert File

formance *Rockin' At the Fillmore* (A&M3506) and 1972's *Smokin'* (A&M 4342) would both go Gold, but it would be a solo album from one of Humble pie's members that would really solidify A&M's standing as one of the decades top labels.

A&M Comes Alive

Peter Frampton had been signed as a solo artist in 1972 and had three well received LP's out by 1976 when he decided to release a live album of material recorded during a 1975 US tour. The result *Frampton Comes Alive* (A&M 3703); was first thought to be aimed at roughly the same audience as Humble Pie. With a buoyant response from AM radio however it was soon evident that the Frampton sound was crossing over to a much younger crowd- with large purchasing power. With these two large record buying sectors *Frampton Comes Alive* was destined to become one of the biggest selling live lp's of all time and would eventually end up with sales figures near 10 million copies.

Other English acts to have hits on A&M Records in the early 1970's included Free and Stealers Wheel. Free, led by future Bad Company vocalist Paul Rodgers gave us the classic FM favorite 'All Right Now' (A&M 1206) in September of 1970. Stealers Wheel meanwhile were fronted by future solo star Gerry Rafferty and notched a pair of Top 40 hits in the early part of the decade, the most popular being 'Stuck In The Middle With You' (A&M 1416), a

The House of A&M

Dylan inspired classic that hit #6 on the US charts in March 1973.

A year later in 1974 saw the A&M signing of keyboardist extraordinaire Rick Wakeman. Having recently quit the group Yes Wakeman was given a free reign to indulge himself in his unique brand of classical instrumentals. Although Wakeman's albums were not all big sellers they demonstrated to the music world that A&M Records were willing to sign acts for their creative merit rather than concentrating solely on just having a hit.

The TJB Returns

Herb Alpert himself knew this only too well, as he would issue a string of LP's in the mid '70's that showed him growing artistically but failing commercially. Having sat on the sidelines for the better part of four years Alpert rather quickly plunged in to a new Tijuana Brass era that emulated the old with a long world tour, network TV specials and black-tie performances before royalty. Unlike the previous TJB incarnation however the 1970's version failed to catch on with the record buying public. In fact many of Alpert's 1970's releases are harder to find than anything he may have put out in the early 1960's and many failed to chart at all on any of the trade publications.

Returning with a bang in the spring of 1974 was a new Tijuana Brass, arriving with new person-

The Herb Alpert File

nel, a new album and U.S. concert tour that would stretch on into the fall. After a very well received opening concert at Lake Tahoe in April and some glowing reviews for his new album, *You Smile-The Song Begins* (A&M 3620) (dedicated to the new Mrs. Alpert, Lani Hall[67]), it seemed the world was ready to be conquered again by Herb Alpert. The new TJB consisted of some top-flight musicians from various backgrounds- Julius Wechter, a long time contributor to many of the 1960's TJB recordings was installed as percussionist (vibes and marimba). Wechter shared the stage with other 1960's alumni- Bob Edmondson on trombone, John Pisano on guitar and ex-Brasil '66 vocalist (and new wife of Herb Alpert) Lani Hall. Augmenting the 'Brass was a crew of jazz session men- the powerful Bob Findley on trumpet, Ernie McDaniel on bass, Dave Frishberg on piano, Vince Charles on steel drums and Steve Schaeffer on drums.

But alas it wasn't to be just yet. The lead track 'Fox Hunt' (A&M1526), arranged by Quincy Jones, died at #70 while the album fell quickly off the charts even before the completion of the TJB world tour. The original excitement of hearing classic 'Brass tracks along with new progressive jazz influenced stuff seemed to have warn off by the end of the summer.

---

[67] Alpert and Hall registered for a marriage in Malibu in January 1974 and were married in March 1974.

The House of A&M

Critic Frances Buglione thought that "Alpert seems to have lost the charm that made his Tijuana Brass one of the country's most celebrated instrumental groups" after a Connecticut concert in late August. Buglione was put off by the new mod '70's look of the 'Brass and stated bluntly that, "The group is larger, hairier, and sloppier."[68] San Mateo's Robert Burmister was equally brutal after a late autumn gig in northern California. He found that the new TJB, "used too much lard" and that Alpert "is apparently still afraid that North American digestive system is too delicate to handle the real thing."[69]

Despite some sour US reviews Alpert would march on through the 1974 tour and taste enough of his past glory to continue on with the new Tijuana Brass on into 1975. Culminating the European tour was a massive concert for Princess Grace at the Palais Champs Elysees in Paris[70]. For one night at least Alpert and his crew were able to shine in the regal limelight they once owned. According to the gossip columns. "Grace and Herb Alpert spent most of the time during intermission talking about Michele Thomas, who taught both of them French. He is a superb tutor, if you listen to Herb and Grace. Even if

---

[68] Bridgeport Post 8/27/74 p.16

[69] San Mateo Times 11/23/74 p9

[70] Alpert's performance was made as a benefit for the Princess Grace of Monaco's Foundation in support of artisans.

The Herb Alpert File

you don't..."[71] This concert was possibly the biggest black-tie affair of Alpert's career with a guest list that included, "Baron Guy de Rothschild, Baron Alexis de Rede, Marc Bohan-the head of the House of Dior, and Rose-marie (Kanzler) and Jean-Pierre Mercie-Riviere." Apparently Mdme Rose-marie's sleeves were so large, "She could have smuggled Herb Alpert right out in them." In Europe at least the Tijuana Brass were still welcomed with open arms.

Back in the US Alpert decided to try a different approach to win back a devoted following: The Muppets! Teaming up with producers Gary Smith and Dwight Hemion, the same duo that had produced his first big special back in 1966, Alpert shared the stage with an unlikely co-star in Kermit the Frog in this 1974 ABC TV Special. Ratings weren't quite what they had been back in the '60's and the show only seemed to give Alpert's critics even more fodder for their diatribes against the TJB leader.

In a rare and detailed interview with syndicated columnist Marilyn Beck *('Herb Alpert Has Lip Back After 5 Years'*[72]) Alpert finally clued in the public as to why he had essentially vanished from the music in 1969. "My lip was gone! The harder I tried, the worse my music got. I'm not sure I understand it completely today, but I loved my horn, and it turned

---

[71] Syracues Herald-Journal,10/14/74 p12'Suzy Says' column

[72] Albequrque Tribune 10/24/74 pF6

The House of A&M

against me. I didn't know if I would even get it back."

Having got so frustrated with his trumpet playing in the early '70's Alpert decided simply to start all over and began taking lessons in New York to get his sound up to snuff. Working under the tutelage of Carmine Caruso, in person and over the phone, Alpert was happy to have turned the corner. "I haven't gotten my lip back entirely yet. But I feel better emotionally than I ever have," Alpert related to Beck, "Caruso has taught me much about the horn- and about life."

The new Tijuana Brass that had begun with such high hopes in the spring of 1974 would finally fizzle out in the summer 1975 with the release of *Coney Island* (A&M 4521), an album that was all but ignored by the music industry at large. Despite a much publicized appearance on the hip late night music program 'Midnight Special'[73], Alpert's second coming of the 'Brass was not connecting at all with the record buying public. As critic William D. Laffler put it in his generally buoyant review of *Coney Island*, "Alpert is Taking It Slow"[74]

Alpert seemed unfazed by this lack of reception by US music fans and seemed to be finally listening to his heart when it came to the *real* impor-

---

[73] Alpert hosted the June 20, 1975 episode of the Midnight Special- which was essentially an A&M special with A&M artists Captain & Tenille, Billy Preston and Supertramp all performing along with the maestro Alpert.

[74] The Denton Record Chronicle 10/16/74 p7A

The Herb Alpert File

tant things in life. After watching the heartbreaking news reports about the plight of Vietnamese "boat people" who had ended up on American shores, Alpert took it upon himself to spread a little happiness. Trudging up to Camp Pendleton, where many refugees were being kept, Alpert performed a joyous concert before some 15,000 refugees, many of them children[75].

In September during a tour of Canada Alpert opened up in a *'Special Event with Winnipeg Symphony'* that reviewer Barbara Cansino felt "had the air of a faculty of a Brass University seminar- presented in live documentary form"[76]. Cansino found that. "Mrs. Alpert has a lovely voice" and "sang an emotionally-intense solo on *'The Way We Were'*". Although Cansino felt that Alpert was generally "not at all funny", she was receptive to his anecdotes about childbirth, ("The Alperts dealt with childbirth creatively together with Herb bathing the baby almost directly after the birth."[77]) and felt the Alperts to be snappy dressers, "Arm in arm together on stage the Alperts make the Cashes (Johnny and June) look jaded."

The Canadian tour had a dark moment however when the flight Alpert and the band had

---

[75] Burlington Times-News p6B 6/24/75

[76] Winnipeg Free Press 9/17/75p34 'Tijuana Brass Masterful' by Barbara Cansino

[77] Aria Alpert was born to the Herb Alpert and Lani Hall in July of 1975.

The House of A&M

boarded from Regina received a telephoned bomb threat. The Associated Press reported, "Flight 226, en route to Winnipeg, turned back 20 minutes after leaving Regina. The plane was searched by Royal Canadian Mounted Police officers and was allowed to resume its flight when nothing was found.'[78]

At the conclusion of the 1975 Alpert was a bit deflated with the demise of the second incarnation of the Tijuana Brass. *Coney Island* and a late autumn single 'Whistle Star' were both commercial failures, leading Alpert to conclude, "There is no more formulas in music, no common denominators for making hit records." Speaking to columnist Vernon Scott, Alpert explained the mid-70's music scene: "it's all open. No more trendy styles. The world is in the hands of artists, not politicians. Parents shouldn't turn away from music their kids dig. It widens the generation gap." Waxing philosophic Alpert declared, "Music could bind the world together because musicians project the temper of the times."[79]

Poor record sales didn't stop the now verbose Herb Alpert from pushing forth with a critically acclaimed solo debut in *Just You and Me* (A&M 4591) in the Bicentennial summer of 1976. Critics found the new Alpert disc, "moodier, much more interest-

---

[78] 'Herb Alpert aboard bomb threatened plane in Canada' (AP) Anderson Daily Bulletin 9/16/74 p2

[79] 'Delayed Comeback for Herb Alpert' by Vernon Scott San Mateo Times 11/1/75 p19

The Herb Alpert File

ing than his Tijuana Brass records"[80] Reviewer Chuck Graham's positive critique felt that Alpert, "has been careful not to add contemporary disco rhythms or other artificial sweeteners" and that the "entire album is full of those touches that lifted the trumpeter from obscurity to fortune nearly fifteen years ago."[81] Record buyers however never found it at all-and *Just You and Me* marked another Alpert release of the '70's to fall into an abyss as the age disco, punk and fusion came to a head.

Herb Alpert- the one-time king of American pop music- was now nowhere to be found. His problem was simple; it would take a long time for him to outgrow the image he created of himself in the 1960's. As critic Lee Marguiles noted, "A lot of people don't seem ready to accept Alpert's new musical stance. A&M executives say a lot of so-called progressive radio stations won't even listen to the solo album because they assume it's full of the TJB sound that they now consider light-weight."[82]

By 1976 the "sixties" seemed like a far off time and artists that were successful then would essentially have to re-invent themselves to be taken seriously in the mid-1970's, unless of course they

---

[80] 'Success Meant Problems, Now Herb Alpert's a Solo' (AP) Indiana Evening Gazette 8/30/76 p22

[81] 'Brassy Alpert Returns' by Chuck Graham, Tucson Daily Citizen 6/22/76 p15

[82] ibid

The House of A&M

wanted to simply wax nostalgic, which Alpert did not.

With other artists like Deodato and Stanley Clarke having both creative and commercial success in the newly christened jazz-fusion genre it was only natural that Alpert, the master of hybrid instrumentals, would gravitate into this field. By 1977 he was working with the like of George Benson, Manolero Badrena and Letta Mbulu- in many ways foreshadowing the "world" music craze of the 1990's.

As usual Alpert also had his keen eye out for new talent and in 1976 he signed the great Argentine sax-man Gato Barbieri to a recording contract on A&M. The resulting album, *Caliente* (A&M) became Barbieri's biggest selling album ever and forged the groundwork for the great jazz pop era (i.e. Weather Report, Spyro Gyra, Angela Bofill et al) that lay ahead.

Foreign Natives

Teaming up with fellow horn player Hugh Masekela for a pair of albums in 1978 Alpert himself would finally begin to emerge from the shadow of his not to be taken serious days of the Tijuana Brass. Both Masekela albums were favorites among the increasing influential jazz crossover world and included contributions from soloists like Lee

The Herb Alpert File

Ritenour (guitar), Bob Findley[83] (trumpet) and Manolo Badrena (percussion)[84]. The concert performance *Main Event-Live* (A&M) remains the only official live release from Alpert in his long career.

While Herb Alpert, the musician, was continuing to find himself in the L.A. session world other A&M acts were selling millions. Following in the footsteps of the reigning soft pop champs The Carpenters was The Captain & Tennille. Beginning with the 1975 # 1 'Love Will Keep Us Together (A&M 1672), The Captain, Daryl Dragon (an ex-Beach Boy) and his wife Toni Tenille notched up five consecutive million sellers in only two years. Eventually Captain & Tenille would place a total of eight hits in the US Top 40 by the decades end before fading.

Rita Coolidge was another million selling artist for A&M in the '70's. After a few less than inspiring collaborations with her husband Kris Kristofferson in the early part of the decade, Coolidge emerged as a major solo act with a pair of Gold singles in 1977 and would continue with chart success (if not critical) throughout the late 1970's and early 1980's.

The Chicago based rock quintet Styx also became a major force in the late '70's and by the end

---

[83] A longtime member of the Tommy Dorsey Band- Findley would contribute greatly to Steely Dan's funk-pop classic 'Royal Scam' in 1976 and contribute to many tv and film soundtracks.

[84] Alpert in fact would produce Badrena's 1978 solo album for A&M

The House of A&M

of 1978 had five hit singles under their belt in addition to four Gold albums. Mainly an FM 'Album oriented Rock' (AOR) attraction Styx would become a supergroup by the decades end, selling out stadiums and arenas. Styx in fact would help A&M close out the decade atop the singles chart with the #1 single 'Babe" (A&M 2188) in December 1979.

Music that was perhaps a bit closer Herb Alpert's heart (i.e. jazzy/pop instrumentals) also made headway commercially in the mid to late '70's with stellar performances from Quincy Jones and Chuck Mangione. Jones had been signed to A&M back in 1969 and had annually come forth with his distinct collection of jazz, pop and funk. He reached perhaps a creative and commercial apex in 1978 with *Sounds...and Stuff Like That.* Fluegel horn player supreme Chuck Mangione saw his records sell extremely well as the decade progressed, even placing one of his instrumental tracks at the top of the singles chart when 'Feels So Good' (A&M 2001) hit # 4 in the spring of 1978.

A&M is Swindled and Punked

Constantly keeping on top of what was the new and hip sound A&M Records made (or attempted to make) major inroads into the punk and new wave world when they became the all the rave in 1977. For a brief period of one week A&M had the then hottest group in the world, The Sex Pistols, under contract. This was during there 'Pistols brief

The Herb Alpert File

U.S. tour and is chronicled in Malcolm McLaren's aptly titled film 'The Great Rock 'n Roll Swindle', as the group never recorded one note for A&M despite receiving an advance of some $80,000.

Another punk group, The Stranglers, had a more productive relationship with A&M after the label secured the U.S. rights to their material in early 1977. Led by guitarist Hugh Cornwell and bassist Jean Burnel the Stranglers were the thinking man's punk outfit, gaining inspiration from Camus and haunting baroque melodies. In '77 they produced two of the greatest albums in the annals of punk, their debut *Rattus Norvetigus IV* and their follow up *No More Heroes* both now hot collectors in their A&M form.

One year later saw the signing of another punk/new wave act, an obscure trio led by a former school teacher, one Gordon Sumner, who went by the single name of "Sting". The band had shown such a determination to make it that they had even paid their own airfare on their first U.S. tour. They called themselves The Police and had previously recorded for a small independent label in England called Illegal Records. They debuted on A&M with the reggae-ish Roxanne (A&M 2096) in late 1978. Although it was a sizable hit few then suspected the success they would eventually attain.

As the year 1979 dawned the music world was in a state of flux; wide ranging styles from disco

The House of A&M

to punk were selling millions and artists both well known and unknown were offering the record buying public distinct sounds of enjoy. Thanks to their shrewd music industry savvy and a little luck A&M Records would remain in the forefront as the 1970's closed.

Keep Your Eye On Me
1979-1994

It's safe to say that if he had wanted to Herb Alpert could have retired from the music world in 1979 and live quite well thank you on the profits generated by A&M Records. But Herb Alpert is not your usual music biz impresario and his quest to re-conquer the music world he once had in his pocket resulted in one of the greatest comeback stories in the history of pop music. As the decade closed Alpert would have finally re-invented himself as a top selling recording star and in the process initiate a successful career as a solo act.

For the pop icon Herb Alpert the decade of the 1970's had been pretty much a wash out. As he watched recording acts that he had developed score hit after hit, Alpert continually struck out failing to break the magical Top 40 barrier between 1971 and 1979. His 1978 collaborations with Hugh Masekela signaled a thaw in his commercial ice age. The studio set *Herb Alpert/Hugh Masekela*

The Herb Alpert File

(A&M/Horizon 118/728) became a moderate seller peaking at around #70 and the live album, *Main Event-Live* (A&M 47Z7), followed with similar results.

But it would be a return to the hit singles chart that would secure Alpert's standing as a pop music giant. Defying the odds Alpert was about to score a monster-hit single in 'Rise' (A&M 2151), a finely crafted instrumental written by his nephew Randy Badazz and his friend Andy Armer. Ironically this track was almost not recorded, as the original idea at the recording session was to record disco versions of old Tijuana Brass hits.

Halfway through re-doing 'The Lonely Bull' Alpert realized that "disco-izing" his old classics wasn't such a great idea after all, with several hours of recording time left for their session Alpert asked his piano playing/composing nephew Badazz if he had any other material to record.

Badazz obliged his uncle with the eventual Grammy winning 'Rise". By July of 1979 when the single was issued, the US charts had been dominated that year by Donna Summer and a plethora of tacky disco hits. Although disco influenced, 'Rise' was yet another hybrid of styles with even a hint of the old Mexican sound coming through on it.

As the summer of '79 progressed there was little hint that Alpert was about to score one of the biggest hits of his career. On August 25th Rise

Keep Your Eye On Me

stood at #45 on the Cashbox chart mainly on the strength of airplay by major AM Radio stations. Few who had heard the song even knew it was Herb Alpert performing it.

But as is the case with many great hit singles Rise had a few quirks of fate to push it along. It got one of its biggest plugs from a very unexpected source- the television soap opera 'General Hospital- during a controversial scene of a woman being pursued by a rapist, hardly the sort of endorsement the mild mannered Alpert would have sought. In any event the song was played several times on the program and undoubtedly had a big effect on the song breaking the Top Ten. Another reason Rise became a big hit was the growing audience of "crossover" music, music that appealed to both black and white listeners.

'Rise' received abundant airplay on black and disco stations in addition to still strong AM Top 40 outlets; these two varied audiences helped propel it to the top of the charts. One station in particular, WBLS-FM in New York, the top rated Urban music station in the country, was seen as the first to add 'Rise' to its play list. And as the Chicago Tribune's Larry Kart noted, "The core audience for 'Rise' seems to be young, black and disco-oriented." Alpert agreed and seemed happy to have found a new younger audience that consisted of. "People

The Herb Alpert File

who probably have no idea of what I've done in the past.[85]"

Alpert himself offered this analysis of pop and disco in a rare interview in late 1979, "I know disco's not the rage anymore. But I also know that lots of people still dance. I wanted to plug into that-not to make another routine disco record, but to take some of th6se elements and come up with something I'd have fun playing. It worked out, '*Rise*' is slower than most disco songs, and so late at night when everybody in the disco is worn out they all get together and dance to it[86]."

Capitalizing on its disco feel Alpert went back into the studio and re-recorded 'Rise' and issued it in a longer version as a 12 inch single (A&M 12022) for club d.j.'s. This was the heyday of disco singles and the popularity of 'Rise' in its new version led for calls for an entire album of new Alpert material. Back again to the studio went Alpert, this time with a group of top-notch session men.

Completed with the likes of Joe Sample (piano), Harvey Mason (drums) and Abe Laboriel (bass) and recorded digitally by engineers Don

---

[85] 'Herb Alpert rises on Charts with Rise' by Larry Kart (Chicago Tribune) 11/9/79

[86] Rolling Stone 12/13/79

Keep Your Eye On Me

Hahn and Mark Smith the album *Rise* (A&M 4790) was a slick up to date pop collage that exemplified very well the new solo Herb Alpert. The LP opened with the Mexican influenced triumphant '1980', a track Alpert had penned for the next years Olympic ceremonies on NBC. It then faded into the new version of 'Rise' (now virtually twice as long as the original single version). A dance flavored 'Behind The Rain' followed and the etheric- almost new wave-ish 'Rotation' closed out side one. A cover of the Crusaders recent hit 'Street Life' and the funky 'Love Is', which saw the return of Herb Alpert the vocalist, highlighted the second side.

After a decade in the wilderness it was a relief to know that he hadn't completely fallen off the radar. "I was consumed by a desire to make popular records again," Alpert confessed, "I missed that kind of success very much, even though I wasn't willing to do just anything to get back on the charts." Invoking the Beatles, Alpert concluded, "And the road back proved to be a long and winding one"[87].

Recording the new album was exhilarating for Alpert as he related to Rolling Stone's Steve Pond in a December 1979 interview: "When I'm in there with a horn in my hand and my ass on the line I try to tap the source, to be adventurous. I want to get to the point where I'm not gonna worry if it's going to sell, or if the drummer likes it, or if the guy behind

---
[87] ibid

The Herb Alpert File

the glass is. digging it. If you can get all that stuff out of your mind, then you can be original, and then you're more likely to come up with that magical phrase"[88].

Whether magic had anything to do with it or not the single 'Rise' meanwhile continued to do just that and broke into the Top 10 in early October. A bunch of first rate singles were also climbing the charts at the time and competition to see who could claim the #1 spot was, for the first time in years, exciting. Pop Muzik by new waver M (Robin Scott), Escape from singer-songwriter Rupert Holmes, Rapper's Delight by New York rap stars The Sugarhill Gang; as well as new material from Kool & The Gang, Michael Jackson, The Eagles and Donna Summer gave the decade of the 1970's a chance to close with a bang.

So in October 1979, as fate would have it exactly 17 years to the day of 'The Lonely Bull's first chart appearance (October 20) Herb Alpert had the top selling record in America. His comeback was complete as *Rise* hit #1 on all trade publications and would soon after be certified Gold for one million copies sold. Once again life, Herb Alpert and A&M Records were in happy harmony together.

And the harmony would continue on into the New Year. and decade. *Rise,* the album, would

---

[88] ibid

Keep Your Eye On Me

climb to #6 and a follow up single, Rotation (A&M 2202), would become a sizable hit on the heels of 'Rise', reaching #28 in February of 1980. Also in February of 1980 came the Grammy Awards with Herb coping an award for 'Rise' as 'best pop instrumental'.

Refusing to stand still on his new found success Alpert delved right back in to recording and would experience one of his most creative periods in the early 1980's. In July of 1980 he emerged from the recording studio with a new single and album both titled *Beyond* (A&M 3717/2246). It would be with this set that Alpert would see his musical categorization shift into a genre that unfortunately ended up being a black hole for his record sales: jazz fusion.

The single 'Beyond' would find a home on jazz pop stations like WRVR in New York and would get little if no airplay on Top 40 radio. Sales for the album were moderate (it reached #28 on Billboard's LP chart) but it was evident that instrumental pop, be it jazz or otherwise, would never attain the constant platinum status of its competitive genres.

As he had in the 1960's Alpert showed little concern for what label his music now fell under and he applied himself diligently on a series of projects that would result in perhaps his most satisfying solo albums. The brilliant *Magic Man* (A&M 3728) was issued in 1981 to critical if not commercial approval and was highlighted by the re-working of the 1974

The Herb Alpert File

track 'You Smile- The Song Begins'. The album's lead single, 'Manhattan Melody (.A&M 2375), was a smooth, slightly funky number, that failed to get any radio support outside a few "urban contemporary" stations in New York and Los Angeles, and as a consequence it failed to make any headway on the pop charts.

By the summer of 1982 however Alpert would be back on the hit parade with 'Route 101' (A&M 2422), a cool' get in your car and drive instrumental that despite competing with a bunch of British new-wavers would hit #37 on Billboard's Hot 100 in July.

The *Fandango* album (A&M 3731) soon followed and was well received by both press and public. Commemorating his twentieth year as a recording star, and twenty years of A&M Records, Fandango had a decidedly Mexican flavor to it, caused in no small part by the fact that the top Mexican song-writer Jose Quintara produced it. It was perhaps Alpert's favorite solo effort and certainly one of his strongest. (This set incidentally is the only one of these early '80's albums to see release on compact disc.)

Nineteen eighty-three's *Blow Your Own Horn* (A&M 4949) was dedicated to the late Karen Carpenter, who's sudden death shocked not only the A&M

Keep Your Eye On Me

family but the entire music industry[89]. This slickly produced set showcased a funkier fusionized Alpert and contained two of his best solo singles, 'Red Hot' and 'Garden Party', neither of which became hits. The LP was a moderate seller and signaled another new beginning for Alpert; his third decade as a performer had begun and the musical chameleon was about to change his spots once again.

One Last Diamond

With the 1984 Olympics being staged in Los Angeles it seemed appropriate to have native son Herb Alpert initiate the ceremonies wth a Tijuana sounding concert at the Greek Theater. After rounding up many of the former TJB members and getting offers to perform from various places around the US Alpert decided to put the Tijuana Brass together one more time.

As Alpert explained to the NY Times Jon Pareles, "I had no intentions of doing another Tijuana Brass tour. We were asked to perform during the Olympics at the Greek Theater in Los Angeles and that sounded exciting. The idea was just to get the guys together and leave it at that, but offers came in from all over the country. I decided, as long

---

[89] Karen Carpenter died of anorexia in February 1983. Alpert was shaken greatly and stated, "Hers was a voice that brought happiness to millions. And It will live with us forever."

The Herb Alpert File

as it's going to take a month of rehearsals to get everybody back in shape, we might as well do it."[90]

Coinciding with the limited 1984 Tijuana Brass tour was the album *Bullish* (A&M 5022), which despite bearing the moniker *Herb Alpert-Tijuana Brass* on the cover-failed to include any TJB members on the songs. While the title track actually broke Billboard's Hot 100 briefly, *Bullish* and it's follow up, *Wild Romance* (A&M 5082) seemed to slip through the cracks of many Alpert fans.

New fresh material from Herb Alpert would come in 1987 with his most significant album of the decade, *Keep Your Eye On Me* (A&M 5125). This album including production help from Jimmy Jam and Terry Lewis, the two dazzling hip hop and funk comrades Minneapolis Sound fame- who had a magic touch of sorts in the late '80's turning every artist they touched into gold. This Herb Alpert project would be no different.

Teaming up with fellow A&M mega-star Janet Jackson (the top seller on A&M in the late '80's) Alpert scored his first top ten hit in eight years with the slick pop dance number 'Diamonds' (A&M 2929), which climbed all the way to #5 on the Billboard Hot 100. In the UK, the title track would turn out to be the big hit, peaking at #19 on the BBC charts.

---

[90] 'Alpert Back at the Bandstand-For A Bit' by Jon Pareles, NY Times 8/29/84

Keep Your Eye On Me

The album *Keep Your Eye On Me* meanwhile returned Alpert to the album charts and would be certified Gold by the end of the summer. Another hit single followed in August, 'Making Love In The Rain' (A&M 2949), a #35 hit that gave Alpert 22 Top 40 hits for his career.

Despite being once again on the charts, Alpert was but a minor act on the A&M roster as the '80's closed. Diverse sounds from UB40, Bryan Adams, Sting and the aforementioned Janet Jackson would turn into platinum hits in the U.S. and abroad and by consequence turn the once small A&M Records into a multi-million dollar enterprise.

In 1988 Alpert switched gears as far as his solo career was concerned and would end the 1980's with a pair of fine sounding albums of a diverse nature. *Under A Spanish Moon* (A&M 5209) continued Alpert's appreciation of Latin music with lavish orchestration and compositions from Sting, Eduardo Del Barrio and Keith Jarrett. Alpert even promoted this extravagant record with a few concert appearances – complete with a symphonic orchestra on an opposite stage.

The 1989 release *My Abstract Heart* (A&M 5273) showed an appreciation for the cool west coast jazz that Alpert had grown up listening too in the early '50's. Featuring jazz legend Shorty Rodgers on flugelhorn and first rate studio men like Abraham Laboriel (bass), Alex Acuna (percussion),

The Herb Alpert File

Harvey Mason (drums) and Eric Gale (guitar), *'Heart* showed Alpert heading back into the jazz direction, albeit peppered with contemporary funk sounds that made it a little more accessible to younger ears.

A&M Sells Out

The age of corporate buyouts would not go unnoticed in the record industry. David Geffen would sell his exclusive Geffen Records to the highest bidder; Columbia and its major affiliated labels would go to Sony. So it was not too surprising to industry insiders that rumors about A&M Records being up for sale to Polygram Records made the rounds in 1988 and 1989.

The year of 1990 was to be a gratifying one for Herb Alpert on several fronts. First came the reassurances from Polygram that A&M and its operations would remain essentially independent and that Alpert and Moss' important roles as active label chairmen would be able to continue unfettered once the sale was completed.

On the music front Alpert was to undertake the production of an album by one of his favorite jazz greats: Stan Getz. Also Alpert himself would also continue his solo output with an unabashed funk pop collection called *North on South* (A&M 5354).

Keep Your Eye On Me

Working with saxophone legend Getz was like a dream come true for Alpert and he worked diligently on the album throughout 1990 readying it for release in early 1991. *Apasianado* was warmly received by the jazz press and spent a great deal of time near the top of the jazz charts after its release.

Sadly Stan Getz would die shortly after the lp's release after a long battle with cancer and alcoholism, making Alpert's collaboration with him that much more poignant. Many years later Alpert would oversee a Verve Records release of Getz' final recordings, made during the *Apasianado* sessions[91], a fitting tribute to the great sax legend.

Alpert would commemorate the 30th anniversary of 'The Lonely Bull' with *Midnight Sun* (A&M 5391), a set especially dedicated to the late Getz. It was Alpert's 33rd LP release since 1962 and featured a re-working of the 1965 hit 'A Taste Of Honey', as well as a track Alpert recorded with Getz titled 'Friends'. *'Sun* was and historic set as it would mark Herb Alpert's final album for A&M Records.

As 1993 dawned it was becoming clear however that an important musical era was indeed coming to an end. With Polygram now making its presence' known in no uncertain terms (longtime label prez Gil Friesen had already called it quits-resigning in early '90 after 25 years at the A&M

---

[91] Bossas and Ballads:The Lost Sessions-Stan Getz (Verve 2003)

The Herb Alpert File

helm) both Alpert and Moss could see the writing on the wall with their independence slipping into corporate reshuffling.

Finally in May of 1993 press reports confirmed the in evitable: both Alpert and Moss were stepping down as active heads of A&M Records. At a Hollywood function Alpert spoke of his long-term partnership and its imminent demise. "My partner Jerry and I started this company on a handshake 31 years ago and it turned into a hug. It's sad to see it winding down after 31 years.[92]" Moss and Alpert would continue on as heads of their music-publishing firm Almo Music and in 1994 word in the industry was that Almo..... would become...an independent record company.

The now A&M free Herb Alpert was about to catch his second wind...and write yet another chapter in his musical career.

---

[92] Billboard Magazine 5/12/93

Second Wind
1995-present

Having issued a series of critically received albums in the early 1990's it may have surprised more than a few people that Herb Alpert would continue to explore musical styles as the decade of grunge, 'Macarena' and Clinton progressed. In fact Alpert was active on many different fronts at once, having produced a major Broadway hit[93] ('Angels In America'), founded a charitable institution (The Herb Alpert Foundation[94]) and guest starred on numerous pop albums from friends like Jim Brickman, Gato Barbieri and Rita Coolidge, to name a few. On the creative front Alpert had also undertaken artistic endeavors and by the mid-1990's had even made a

---

[93] Alpert's production of Tony Kushner's Angels in America even won a Tony award in 1990

[94] In the 1980s he created The Herb Alpert Foundation and the Alpert Awards in the Arts with The California Institute of the Arts (CalArts). The Foundation supports youth and arts education as well as environmental issues and helps fund the PBS series "Bill Moyers on Faith and Reason."

The Herb Alpert File

name for himself as a sculptor and a major patron of the arts.

Catching A Second Wind

As he had done some two decades before Alpert teamed up with a prominent jazz player to reignite his solo career; in this case Jeff Lorber, a highly regarded jazz fusion keyboardist from Philadelphia. Yet unlike previous solo sojourns Alpert decided to support his new music with a full-fledged tour and over a two year period performed in a series of well received US and European concerts before undertaking his first ever Montreux appearance.[95]

Aptly title *Second Wind* Herb Alpert's first release on Almo Records was a funky masterpiece that echoed some of Miles Davis' later Warner releases. Bringing to life some of the best elements of both hip hop and some of the classic fusion of the 1970's, think Jimmy Jam meets Weather Report, *Second Wind* was a remarkable solid set that stood up as a perfect bookend to 1979's *Rise*, capping a decade and a half of Herb Alpert's version of smooth jazz.

Lorber's presence gave Alpert's funk attempts direction and worked well in concert. Lorber's band even brought life to some of Alpert's older material in concert as is evident in their appearance at the

---

[95] Alpert's Montreux performance was eventually issued on DVD in 1996 on Eagle Eye Media and shows the band in fine form on cuts like 'Rise', 'The Lonely Bull' and 'Sugar Cane'.

Second Wind

1996 Montreux Jazz Festival. This rare Alpert concert was videotaped and eventually issued on a DVD in 2006, showing that Alpert had lost none of his ability as a top showman and performer. Highlights of this show include a groovy 8-minute rendition of 'Rise', a hilarious on-the-spot rendition of 'Spanish Flea' and a poignant encore of 'This Guy's In Love With You'.

With such a fine comeback under his belt one might have assumed Alpert would lie low for a bit. Instead in 1997 Alpert was back again with another fine collection of instrumental pop fusion. *Passion Dance* was Alpert's Mexican comeback and was a set especially dedicated to all the old TJB fans. Soon after it's release Alpert received confirmation of his Latin appreciation by receiving the Billboard International Latin Music Lifetime Achievement Award in Miami on April 30.

Passion Dance was a groove-driven hybrid of Latin and Mexican jazz-pop, aided in no small part by co-producer/bassist/keyboardist Oskar Cartaya. Recorded at sessions in LA and Puerto Rico Jazz bible Down Beat was enthusiastic and felt that,"...the arrangements sparkle and the rhythms crackle.... Alpert's playing is jazzier than usual..." Jazz Times also saw *Passion Dance* as a triumph for TJB trumpet-man and declared,[96]- "...anyone seeking hard-hitting, elemental Latin romps will be entranced....Alpert is clearly enjoying himself here..."

---

[96] JazzTimes (10/97, pp.76-77)

The Herb Alpert File

The solo Alpert seemed to have finally taken his playing up a notch, to a level that even satisfied his own high personal demands. In June of 1999 Alpert completed his late-90's trilogy with *Colors*- another stellar, well-crafted set that featured the Grammy nominated 'The Look of Love'. Co-produced by the great Living Colour drummer Will Calhoun, *Colors* also got vocal support from Lani Hall aka Mrs. Herb Alpert and a well-seasoned bunch of session players.

Remastered and Re-Whipped

The 21st Century Herb Alpert saga has been one of appreciation for the Tijuana Brass, as virtually the entire 1960's catalogue has been remastered and issued on cd for the first time. The new millennium has also seen Alpert take another stab at being up-to-date and hip, with the release of striking remix album of the 1965 lp *Whipped Cream & Other Delights*.

In the year 2000, Herb Alpert bought back the rights to his music from Universal[97] who had shamelessly dismantled the entire A&M operation and had basically turned A&M Records into an imprint of UMG. With the precious and historical master tapes in hand Alpert along with engineer Ted Jensen of Sterling Sound, began remastering his albums for CD reissue, many of them appearing on cd in fact for the very first time.

---

[97] Alpert and Moss also sold their publishing house Rondor Music to Universal in 2000.

Second Wind

In 2005, Shout! Factory, a cutting edge music and film firm headed by Rhino Records co-founder Richard Foos, began distributing digitally remastered versions of Alpert's A&M library to popular acclaim. In addition to the old bestsellers Alpert decided to compile a new album, *Lost Treasures*, which consisted of unreleased material from the TJB era as well as early Alpert solo recordings of the 1970's. In total *Lost Treasures* added some 22 new songs to the Tijuana Brass story and made millions of die-hard TJB fans ecstatic one more time.

For a younger and perhaps hipper crowd Alpert unveiled, in the spring of 2006, a remixed version of the entire *Whipped Cream* album, entitled *Whipped Cream and Other Delights: Re-Whipped*. To some of course this was a sacrilege, as it seemed to be destroying what was deemed a sonic Larry Levine masterpiece. The reality however was that this melding of dj's and TJ's was a brilliant move and was done right. *Re-whipped* was funky and had an edge and echoed all that one liked in the rhythms of that merry bunch of TJB players of four decades before. And oh yeah it sold well too and climbed to #5 on the Billboard Contemporary Jazz chart.

The parent album *Whipped Cream & Other Delights* was also a big hit when issued and hit #1 on the CD Universe chart, giving Alpert hit albums in four consecutive decades!

Still in good health and good looks Alpert undertook a series of well-received concerts in his native LA in the spring of 2007. Along with his wife

The Herb Alpert File

Lani Hall, Alpert and a stellar crew of LA session men jazzed up the small LA club Vibrato in May of '07 in front of a standing room only crowd.

In November of 2007 Herb Alpert, concerned with the current state of music education, decided to back up his concern in a big way, a very big way. In donating some $30 million to UCLA Herb Alpert was providing the funding to encourage music education in the ever changing world of the 21st Century music industry.

"The landscape of music has changed so dramatically in the last few years and the ways of making, delivering and sharing music have become so diverse, there needs to be a new approach to music education," Alpert, declared at a press conference outside Schoenberg Hall, where the UCLA Herb Alpert School Of Music will be located[98].

Now in his early 70's, Herb Alpert has graced the record industry for some 45 years as a hit-maker, showman, solo artist, producer, arranger and much, much more.

In an industry ruled by ego and indulgence Herb Alpert has led by a different example of refinement, humility and rhythm.

Like a magician and troubadour of old he has managed to conjure up wonderment before our very

---

[98] "Herb Alpert pledges $30 to UCLA" AP Wire 11/16/07

Second Wind

eyes and ears. By realizing his own sense of style he has been able to make his own version of the American dream come true.

Thankfully Herb Alpert has allowed us to be part of that dream.
Ole'!

Stephen Vincent O'Rourke

Singapore
April 2008

Appendixes

Appendixes
Discography
TV Appearances
Chronology
Bibliography

The Herb Alpert File

Tijuana Brass

45-RPM Singles

Year	Title	Catalogue Number	Highest Chart #
1962	The Lonely Bull (Twinkle Star)/ Ride, Ride, Ride	A&M 703	-
1962	The Lonely Bull / Acapulco 1922	A&M 703	6
1963	Marching Thru Madrid	A&M 706	-
1963	Let It Be Me	A&M 711	-
1963	Spanish Harlem	A&M 721	-
1963	Mexican Drummer Man	A&M 732	96
1964	Mexican Shuffle	A&M 742	-
1964	El Presidente (Winds Of Barcelona)	A&M 751	-
1964	South Of The Border	A&M 755	-
1965	Whipped Cream	A&M 760	70
1965	Mae	A&M 767	-
1965	A Taste Of Honey/3rd man Theme	A&M 775	1
1965	Tijuana Taxi /Zorba	A&M 787	8

Appendixes

	The Greek (live)		
1966	What Now My Love/Spanish Flea	A&M 792	3
1966	The Work Song	A&M 805	18
1966	Flamingo	A&M 813	28
1966	Mame/Our Day Will Come	A&M 823	19
1967	Casino Royale	A&M 824	1
1967	Wade In The Water/Mexican Road Race	A&M 840	4
1967	The Happening	A&M 860	32
1967	A Banda	A&M 870	1
1967	Carmen	A&M 890	-
1968	Cabaret	A&M 925	-
1968	This Guy's In Love With You	A&M 929	1
1968	Yo Soy Ese Amor (This Guy's In Love With You)	A&M 960	-
1969	The Christmas Song/My Favourite Things	A&M 1001	-
1969	To Wait For Love	A&M 964	36
1969	My Favorite Things	A&M 1015	-
1969	Let It Be Me	A&M 1021	-
1969	Monday, Monday	A&M 1028	-
1969	Zazueira	A&M 1043	-
1970	Jerusalem	A&M 1225	74
1971	Summertime	A&M 1261	-
1971	Darllin'	A&M 1284	-
1973	Last Tango In Paris	A&M 1420	-

The Herb Alpert File

1974	Fox Hunt	A&M1526	-
1974	Save The Sunlight	A&M1542	-
1974	Spanish Harlem	A&M 1586	-
1975	I Belong	A&M 1632	-
1975	Coney Island	A&M 1688	-
1975	Whistle Star	A&M 1762	-

Herb Alpert Solo 45's

Year	Title	A&M Cat.#	Chart #
1977	The You In Me	1962	-
1979	Rise	2151	1
1979	Rotation	2202	30
1979	Street Life	2221	-
1980	Beyond	2246	50
1980	The Continental	2289	-
1980	Kamali	2268	-
1981	Magic Man	2356	-
1981	Manhattan Melody	2375	-
1982	Route 101	2422	37
1982	Fandango	2441	-
1983	Garden Party	2562	-
1983	Red Hot	2593	77
1983	Noche De Amor	35017	-
1984	Bullish	2655	22
1987	Keep Your Eye on Me	2915	3
1987	Diamonds	2929	1
1987	Making Love In the Rain	2949	7
1989	3 O'Clock Jump	1446	59
1991	North On South	1546	40

Appendixes

Tijuana Brass and Herb Alpert LP's and CD's

Year	Title	A&M Cat.#	Chart #
1962	The Lonely Bull	101	24
1964	Volume 2	103	17
1964	South Of The Border	108	6
1965	Whipped Cream & Other Delights	110	1
1966	Going Places	112	1
1966	What Now My Love	114	1
1966	S.R.O.	117	2
1967	Sounds Like…	124	1
1967	Casino Royale Soundtrack	Colgms 5005	22
1967	Herb Alpert's Ninth	134	4
1968	The Beat of The Brass	146	1
1968	The Christmas Album	4166	1
1969	Warm	4190	28
1969	Best Of (promo)	19004	-
1970	The Brass Are Comin'	4228	30
1970	Greatest Hits	4245	-

The Herb Alpert File

1971	Summertime	4314	**61**
1972	Solid Brass	4341	-
1972	Cabaret	Myfr 51034	-
1973	Portrait	4001	-
1973	Foursider	3521	-
1974	You Smile–The Song Begins	3620	**74**
1974	Greatest Hits (Quad)	54245	-
1974	Whipped Cream (Quad)	54110	-
1975	Standards of Today	8007	-
1976	Coney Island	4521	-
1976	Just You & Me	4591	-
1977	Greatest Hits Vol. 2	4627	-
1978	Herb Alpert/Hugh Masekela	H728	-
1978	Main Event Live	4727	-
1979	Rise	4790	**6**
1980	Beyond	3717	**28**
1980	Rise (original master)	MF 1053	
1981	Magic Man	3728	
1982	Fandango	3731	
1983	Blow Your Own Horn	4949	**17**
1984	Bullish	5022	-
1985	Wild Romance	5082	**151**
1987	Keep Your Eye On Me	5125	**5**
1987	Classics Vol. 1	2501	-
1988	Under A Spanish Moon	5209	
1989	Classic Vol20	2518	
1990	The Very Best Of	B0006TIL	

Appendixes

1991	North On South	5345	51
1992	Midnight Sun	5391	14
1996	Second Wind	Almo80005	5
1997	Passion Dance	Almo80014	7
1999	Colors	Almo4949	25
2001	Definitive Hits	8862	3
2005	Lost Treasures	SH32867	-
2006	Re-Whipped.....	SH 97641	2

Chart positions taken from Billboard, Cashbox, Billboard Adult Contemporary, Billboard Hot R&B Hits and Billboard Contemporary Jazz Charts

The Herb Alpert File

Herb Alpert and Tijuana Brass UK Hits

1963	Lonely Bull	Stateside 138	22
1965	Spanish Flea	Pye 25335	3
1966	Tijuana Taxi	Pye25352	37
1967	Casino Royale	A&M 700	27
1968	This Guy's In Love With You	A&M 727	3
1969	Without Her	A&M 755	36
1970	Jerusalem	A&M 810	42
1979	Rise	A&M 7465	13
1980	Rotation	A&M 7500	46
1987	Keep Your Eye On Me	BreakoutUSA 602	19
1987	Diamonds	BreakoutUSA 605	27

Chart positions taken from BBC World Service

Appendixes

The UK version of 'The Lonely Bull' appeared on Stateside Records in 1962.

The UK re-issue of 'Tijuana Brass Vol.2' featured a rare cover shot of the touring ensemble.

This early '70's album was a Europe-only release.

TV Appearances by Herb Alpert

As A Performer:
The Hollywood Palace –1965, 1966, 1967, 1970
The Ed Sullivan Show – 1965. 1968
The Danny Kaye Show – 1965, 1966
The Andy Williams Show - 1966 (2 episodes)
Kraft Music Hall –1967
What's My Line? –1967
Rowan & Martin's Laugh-In - Episode #16- 1968
Soul Train - 1978, 1979, 1984
The Midnight Special – 1975, 1976, 1978
Make Your Own Kind of Music-1971

As a Guest:
The Red Skelton Show (1968)
The Dean Martin Show (1970)
The Dinah Shore Show (1974)
The Mike Douglas Show (1974)
The Today Show (1980)
20/20 (1980)
Later with Bob Costas (1991)

Herb Alpert Appendixes

<u>Special appearances:</u>
The 23rd Annual Grammy Awards (1981)
Special Olympics (1978)
The Brass Are Comin' (1969)
Mr. Hobbs Takes a Vacation (1962) - As the trumpet Player
The Ten Commandments (1956) - As the drummer
Love Me or Leave Me (1955) -As the trumpet Player
The Beat of the Brass (1968)
Herb Alpert & the Tijuana Brass (1966)
Rowan and Martin at the Movies
Say One For Me - Trumpet Player
The Sentry Herb Alpert & the Tijuana Brass Special
Herb Alpert's My Abstract Heart VH1:
Viva Miami

The Herb Alpert File

A HERB ALPERT CHRONOLOGY

1957-Herb Alpert teams begins a partnership with Lou Adler, another aspiring entrepeneur, in the Los Angeles pop music community, as a songwriting team and understudy producers for Keen Records.

1958-Herb Alpert receives his first royalty check for $2.48 for co-writing, "Bim Sam" by Sam Butera & The Witnesses.

Alpert and Adler produce Jan & Dean's "Baby Talk." The record hits the US Top IO.

Alpert and Adler produce the single, "Love, Love, Love," for Lou Rawls and then team with Sam Cooke to write the pop standard, "Wonderful World." Cooke's version of the song reaches the Top 20..

1959- The Herbie Alpert Sextet release the single,

Herb Alpert Appendixes

'*Hully Gully*', on Andex Records.

Jerry Moss, a Bronx native, begins working as a record promotion man for Coed Records. With Moss' help The Crests, '*Sixteen Candles*' climbs to #2 on the pop charts.

1960- Alpert and Adler produce a Top 20 hit with vocalist Don Drowty: Dante & The Evergreens' version of "Alley-Oop for Madison Records.

After Madison Records folds, Alpert and Adler embark on separate careers. Adler eventually founds Dunhill Records in the mid-60's.

Herb signs with RCA Records as a vocalist under the name of Dore Alpert and records several unsuccessful tracks with producer Dick Pierce.

Jerry Moss relocates to Los Angeles and forms a music publishing company called Irving Music.

1961-Herb records the vocal, "Tell it to the Birds," but doesn't release the single until July 1962.

1962-Alpert and Drowty team up with Moss to record 'Hooray for the Big Slow Train', a song to commemorate the 1962 Seattle Worlds Fair.

Herb Alpert and Jerry Moss pool their resources and form Carnival Records, named after the Broadway musical of the period. Alpert's vocal, '*Tell*

The Herb Alpert File

It To The Birds' is issued on July 25, 1962 and is a local hit.

Wink Martindale's Dot Records buys the master tape of *'Tell It To the Birds'* from Carnival Records for $750.

When a title search reveals three other Carnival Records, Alpert and Moss change their company's name to A&M.
A&M Records' first release, The Tijuana Brass single, "The Lonely Bull," breaks onto the westcoast pop charts in August and reaches the US national Top 10 in December.

"The Lonely Bull," enters the pop album chart in December and climbs into the Top 30.

1963-The album, "Herb Alpert & The Tijuana Brass Vol. 2," is released.

Herb Alpert co-produces 3 singles for A&M: "I'm Just a Country Boy," by George McCurry, "Little White Lies," by the Kenjolars and 'The French Song," by Lucille Starr.

Follow up singles by the Tijuana Brass fail to break the US Top 40.

1964-The "South of the Border" album is released and the single, "The Mexican Shuffle" enters the

Herb Alpert Appendixes

pop singles chart. Alpert re-records the song for the Clark Chewing Gum Co.

A&M Records hires Gil Friesen of Capitol Records, Jolene Burton formerly of Liberty Records and engineer Larry Levine, former partner of Phil Spector.

The debut album from the Baja Marimba Band, led by Alpert session partner Julius Wechter, is issued by A&M Records.

1965-At the urging of Gil Friesen Alpert puts together a permanent Tijuana Brass lineup in March and sets out on a nation wide tour.

The Tijuana Brass hits big with "*Whipped Cream*," a sexy Instrumental composition. For a follow-up, A&M releases Herb's version of Anton Kara's "*3rd Man Theme*." The single climbs half-way up the Hot 100 before radio discovers the flip side. Herb's definitive version of the much recorded "*A Taste Of Honey*." This becomes the new "A" side, and zooms to the Top IO in November.

In December, Herb and A&M receive their first two gold albums for, "Whipped Crean And Other Delights" and "Going Places." By the end of the year, "Whipped Cream And Other Delights" is the No. I album in the country and "Going Places" is No. 4 on its way to No. 1.Both albums are on the chart for more than three years, as does the 1964 Tijuana Brass release, "South Of The Border."

The Herb Alpert File

Herb co-produces two Baja Marimba Band albums, "Baja Marimba Band Rides Again," and "For Animals Only."

1966-"Herb Alpert's Tijuana Brass Vol. 2", an album that was actually recorded three years earlier, is re-re-issued and climbs the lp charts.

Herb Alpert & The Tijuana Brass hold down the No. I spot on Billboard's pop album chart for a total of 18 weeks during 1966, more than any other act that year. For 4 of the 18 weeks, the Brass has both the No. I and No. 2 albums. In April, the Brass have four albums in the Top 10 simultaneously. It remains the greatest domination of the Top I0 since the mono and stereo album charts were combined in 1963. Herb Alpert & The Tijuana Brass are listed in the Guiness Book of World Records for having five albums in the Top 20 simultaneously, a feat unequalled in recording history.

The Brass', "What Now My Love," album is released in May and hits No. I in just three weeks. The album holds the top spot for nine weeks, longer than any other album that year. The album is certified gold on May 9, along with three other albums by Alpert and the Brass.

Herb wins four Grammy Awards for "A Taste Of Honey." Record of the Year, Best Instrumental Per-

Herb Alpert Appendixes

formance, Best Instrumental Arrangement and Best Engineered Recording. Herb is also nominated for Album of the Year, for "Whipped Cream And Other Delights."

The National Association of Recording Merchandisers (NARM) singles out "Whipped Cream And Other Delights" as the best-selling album of 1965.

Herb Alpert and Jerry Moss buy the Charlie Chaplin Studios in Hollywood from CBS as A&.M Records' new home.-

The Tijuana Brass release the album, "S.R.O."

Herb Alpert produces the album "Herb Alpert Presents Sergio Mendes & Brasil '66" and co-produces "Watch Out" by Baja Marimba Band.

Alpert also co-produces 3 singles for Chris Montez, "The More I See You," "Call Me" and "Hey Baby."

Herb Alpert initializes a new concept in the music world. He is the first artist to take his group on the road with his own complete sound system.

Herb Alpert has six Top 30 singles this year alone. Among them: title songs for the films "Zorba The Greek" and "Mame," and the peppy Instrumental "Spanish Flea," which later gains fame as the theme from 'The Datinq Game." Biilboard magazine names Herb Alpert "Record Man Of The Year".

The Herb Alpert File

1967-The Tijuana Brass perform at the White House for President Johnson and President Diaz Ordaz of Mexico.

Herb Alpert & The Tijuana Brass' first TV special airs on CBS in April.

Herb Alpert is nominated for four Grammy Awards for "What Now My Love" Including A!bum and Record of the year. He wins - Best Pop Instrumental and Best Instrumental Arrangement.

The Tijuana Brass land their fourth No.1 with "Sounds Like" which zooms into the top spot in just three weeks. The album's big hit, *'Casino Royale'*, is featured in the film of the same name and is the first Tijuana Brass hit composed by Hal David and Burt Bacharach.

Herb Alpert produces another single for Chris Montez, "Because. of You," and co-produces two Baja Marimba Band albums, "Heads up"

1968-Alpert lands his first #1 hit as a vocalist with 'This Guys In Love With You', it's also the first # I hit for the songwriting team of Burt Bacharach and Hal David.
The new 'Brass album, "The Beat of The Brass hits #1 on the album charts upon release in July.

Herb Alpert Appendixes

Alpert sings 'This Guy...' on the CBS-TV special program "Beat of The Brass"

The Tijuana Brass' "Christmas Album", featuring the Top 40 hit 'My Favorite Things', hits #1 on Billboards Seasonal lp chart in December.

1969-The Tijuana Brass play a Royal Command Performance for Queen Elizabeth at the London Palladium.

Another television special, 'The Brass Are Coming' airs on CBS-TV and spawns yet another Top 40 album.

After completing the album 'Warm' and touring the US and UK in the autumn, Alpert announces that he is retiring from live performances.

1970-Alpert helps launch The Carpenters career, collaborating with them on the Bacharach and David song 'Close To You', a US #1 hit.

1971-Alpert releases the critically acclaimed album "Summertime" which features his wife Lani Hall (ex-Brasil '66) on vocals.

1972-Alpert issues "Solid Brass" and produces Lani Hall's debut solo set, "Sundown Lady"

1973-Alpert collaborates with Quincy Jones on the title track to 'Last Tango In Paris'.

The Herb Alpert File

The comprehensive Tijuana Brass compilation "Foursider" is issued by A&M Records

1974-Alpert is married to Lani Hall in March, at a private ceremony in Malibu
After a five year hiatus Alpert re-forms the Tijuana Brass with a new album ("You Smile-The Song Begins") and a tour of the US. A tv special featuring the newly formed Brass airs on ABC-TV.

1975-When the album "Coney Island" bombs, the Tijuana Brass break-up. Alpert begins work on a solo album, "Just You and Me".

1978-Alpert begins a two-year collaboration with Hugh Masekela. A brilliant live album, "Main Event-Live" is issued in early 1979 and charts on the US Jazz charts.

1979-Alpert produces "Manolo" by percussionist Manolo Bandrena.
Herb Alpert's solo career re-ignites itself with the monster hit single 'Rise' which hits #1 in October.

A&M Records begins to have its products distributed by RCA Records distribution network.

1980-The album "Rise' hits #6 and is certified Platinum. Alpert cops a Grammy for the single 'Rise' and has another Top 40 hit with 'Rotation'.

Herb Alpert Appendixes

1982-Alpert scores his final instrumental Top 40 hit with 'Route 101' which is taken from the classy album "Fandango".

1984-The final Tijuana Brass album, "Bullish" is issued and the band does a brief tour of the US.

1987-Alpert collaborates with hip-hop producers Jimy Jam and Terry Lewis and mega-star Janet Jackson on the Gold album "Keep Your Eye on Me".

1988-Alpert releases the album "Under a Spanish Moon", a collaboration with the Los Angeles Philharmonic Orchestra.

1990-Alpert produces Stan Getz' final album "Apasionado".
Alpert and Moss sell A&M Records, the world's largest independent record company, to Polygram Records.
1992-Alpert releases his final album on A&M Records: Midnight Sun.

1993-Both Alpert and Moss retire from their posts at A&M Records. Now a prolific painter, Alpert has his works on display at prestigeous galleries in Europe. Alpert co-produces the Broadway hit "Angels In America"

1995-Jerry Moss and Herb Alpert launch a new la-

The Herb Alpert File

bel, Almo Records.

1996-Alpert collaborates with fusion keyboardist Jeff Lorber on the funky set "Second Wind". Alpert performs a few concerts in LA, NY and San Francisco.

1997-"Passion Dance", a Tijuana Brass inspired set puts Herb Alpert back on the US Jazz charts. Highlights on the cd include a cover of Stevie Wonder's 'Creepin' and a re-working of Herb's 1982 hit 'Route 101'.

1999-Alpert releases the classy set "Herb Alpert and Colors", a collaboration with jazz session players.

2000-Herb Alpert is given an Honorary Doctorate at the famed Berklee School of Music in Boston.
Alpert and Moss sell the publishing house, Rondor Music, to Universal for some $200 million.

Alpert secured the master tapes of all of his recordings- including solo and TJB discs.

2004-In collaboration with Verve Records, Alpert helps issue some of the last recordings of the great Stan Getz.

2005-Shout Factory Records begins releasing the Tijuana Brass catalogue in remastered and digi-pak

Herb Alpert Appendixes

form.

A compilation of lost recordings, "Lost Treasures" issued by Shout Factory.

'Whipped Cream & Other Delights' hits #1 on the CD Universe website.

2006- Alpert is back on the jazz charts with a collaboration with top club dj's entitled Re-Whipped'. The cd hits #2 on Billboard's Contemporary Jazz chart.

Alpert and Moss are inducted into the Rock 'n Roll Hall of Fame for their work at A&M Records.

2007- Alpert and Lani Hall play a week of sold out shows at Vibrato in Los Angeles.

Rise is remastered and issued by Shout Factory.

2008- Alpert and Hall appear on the new album from Sergio Mendes on Concorde Records, *Canto.*

Alpert and Hall play a series of concerts in New York and Los Angeles.

The Herb Alpert File

A Selected Herb Alpert Bibliography

1960's

Daily Northwestern (Oshkosh) 12/27/62 p20 'Nation's Top 10'- Lonely Bull is listed at #1
Winnipeg Free Press 1/19/63 p28 'Disk Data' by Gene Telpner
Independent (Pasadena) 5/21/65 p14 'Alpert Band Joins Miller'- notes upcoming concert as opening act for Roger Miller
Pasadena Star-News 9/2/65 pA-5 'Tijuana Brass Set For Hollywood Bowl Engagement'

Herb Alpert Appendixes

Sunday Post-Crescent 11/7/65 p.15 'Latest Album of Herb Alpert's TJB Demonstrates Group's Matured Style' by David Wagner
Time 11/12/65

AP Wire 1/14/66 'Alpert Mixes US Jazz with Mariachi Beat' by Bob Thomas
The News (Van Nuys) p22A 1/21/66 'Herb Alpert Hits It Big With Fresh New Sound' by Penny Bleile

The News (Van Nuys) p38A 1/28/66 'Leader of Tijuana Brass Gives Teenagers Advice' by Penny Bleile
Variety 3/2/66 'A&M Label Hit Brassy $7.6 million Gross in '65 up 1200%'
Express and News 4/2/66 p9-N 'Herb's Cool Horn Is Real Hot Item'

Newsweek 4/25/66 'Horns of Plenty'
The Daily Review (Hayward, CA) 5/1/66 p7 sec.2 'Platter Parade'
The Abilene Reporter-News 5/8/66 p6 'Bull Market For Tijuana' by Clay Gowarn
The Lowell Sun 5/9/66 p24 'Nobody Sells Like the Tijuana Brass' by Mary Campbell
The Daily Review (Hayward, CA) 5/15/66 p15 TV Week 'Tijuana Brass-Six Million Albums'
NY Daily News 5/29/66
Coronet 6/66 p58
Look 6/14/66 p.104
The Oakland Tribune 6/20/66 p25 'The Brass Glitters' by Bob Thomas

The Herb Alpert File

Idaho State Journal 8/18/66 p31 'Herb Alpert Broke The Sound Barrier to Tune of $-Mollions' by Hal Boyle

Variety 9/7/66
NY Times 9/18/66 'Ole! Here Comes The Tijuana Brass!' by John S. WIlson

New York Times 9/23/66 *p.43'Weather a Wet Blanket For 'Brass on the Grass'*

NEA Syndicated 11/13/66 'Alpert Blows Horn of Plenty' by Joan Crosby

The Post (Frederick, MD)p13 9/16/66 'Herb Alpert Has Bullfight to Thank for His Success' by Joan Crosby

Billboard 12/24/66 'Herb Alpert: Record Man of the Year'
The Daily Gleaner (NV) 3/1/67 'Herb Alpert Tuned in to the Public' by Donald Freeman

The Valley Independent 4/18/67 p23 'Trumpeter Alpert blows the sweet tune of success by Jim Forkan

Independent Star News *(Pasadena)*4/22/67 TV Week

The Coshocton Tribune (Ohio) 5/19/67 p6 'Herb

Herb Alpert Appendixes

Alpert's Music Is Lasting' by Mike Dungjen

UPI 6/17/67 'TJ Brass Revolutionizes Music

New castle News (PA) 6/22/67 'TJB Pianist Lou Pagani returns Home' by John Manka
International Musician 9/67

Town Crier 9/9/67 p30 'Alpert Brass Wails Tonight'

The San Antonio Light 9/10/67 p10-F 'Alpert, Satchmo Team'
Current Biography 1967 Annual

Winnipeg Free Press 4/19/68 p7 'Brass Hour Special In Color on CBC-TV

The Lima News (AZ)4/20/68 p12 'Sharon Is Woman Behind Alpert Notes'

NEA Syndication 4/20/68 'Herb Alpert Rocks Ellis Island with his Brass' by Joan Crosby

UPI Syndication 4/24/68 'The Tijuana Brass' by Rick Dubrow

Gazette-Mail 7/29/68 'Millionaire, Herb Alpert On top as Singer' by Leonard Feather (LA Times syndication)
MelodyMaker 8/3/68

AP Wire 8/17/68 'Alpert's Singing Liked Best' by

The Herb Alpert File

Mary Campbell

Pacific Stars & Stripes 8/20/68 p14 'Herb Alpert Rode Lonely Bull to Brass Ring' by Edgar Reynolds
MelodyMaker 9/7/68

The Daily Tribune (KS) 4/30/69 p8 'People In the News'- notes the Alperts separation

San Antonio Express News 7/13/69 p10 'Herb Alpert Shows Magic Still There' by Jeff Duffield

The Daily Tribune (KS) 7/25/69 'Summer Brings Cloudburst of New Records' by Mary Campbell

The Coshocton Tribune (Ohio) 8/20/69 p6 'Warm by Tijuana Brass is must for Alpert Fans' by William D. Laffler

News Journal (OH) 9/23/69 8-D 'Alpert Turns Brass To Gold' by Cynthia Lowry

The Abilene Reporter News 10/26/69 p12-E 'Tijuana Brass Special Bash Airs Wednesday'

1970's

Billboard 1/24/70 'Alpert Group Disbands:Marimba Cancels PA's'

The Daily Gleaner (NV) 1/26/70 'End of Tijuana Brass' by Marilyn Beck

Herb Alpert Appendixes

Variety 2/11/70 'TJB quits Concerts'

AP Syndication 2/17/70 'Herb Alpert, Brass Take Break'To Watch Hair Grow'"

Pacific Stars & Stripes 5/8/71 p14 'A New Symphony That's Rock-Pop' by Leonard Feather

Rolling Stone 10/12/72 p119 'Two Lonely Bulls & How They Grew' by Judith Sims

The Abilene Reporter 3/24/74 p4-B 'Five Years Since Last Alpert Tour'

Waterloo Courier (IA) 4/17/74 p17 'Herb Alpert Is Returning-His Horn Tried To Tell Him Something' by Bob Thomas

Oakland Tribune 4/23/74 p24 'NiteSounds' by Perry Phillips

The Times (CA) 5/16/74 p17 'Successful Comeback For Alpert by Vernon Scott

The Salt Lake Tribune 5/19/74 p6E 'Herb Alpert and Brass sport new sound' by William S. Welt

Pacific Stars & Stripes 5/21/74 p14 'Wedding March To Play for Alpert'

The Chronicle Telegraph (OH) 7/15/74 p 1 'Even The heavens Clapped' by Ellen Ensel

The Bridgeport Post 8/27/74 p16 'Herb Alpert, Ti-

The Herb Alpert File

juana Brass disappointing to Post Critic' by France Buglione

Albuquerque Tribune 10/24/74 pF-6 'Alpert Has Lip Back After Five Years' by Marilyn Beck

The Times (CA) 11/23/74 'A Watery Alpert Sound for Circle Star Show' by Robert Burmister

The Oakland Tribune 4/13/75 p29-E 'Herb Alpert Opens At Lake Tahoe by Perry Phillips

Independent Press-Telegram (CA) 6/20/75 C-10 'Herb Alpert To Debut on Midnight Special' by Bob Martin

Winnipeg Free Press 9/17/75 p34 'Herb Alpert Masteful' by Barbara Cansino

The Denton Record-Chroncle (TX) 10/16/75 p7A 'Herb Alpert Takes It Slow' by William D.Laffler

The San Mateo Times 11/1/75 p19 'Delayed Comeback For Herb Alpert' by Vernon Scott

Tucson Daily Citizen 6/22/76 p15 'Brassy Alpert Returns' by Chuck Graham

Journal-News (OH) 8/24/76 p19 'Herb Alpert Launches New Career On His Own' by Lee Mar-

Herb Alpert Appendixes

guiles

New Journal (OH) 3/2/77 p17 'Does The Name Herb Alpert Ring A Bell?'

Rolling Stone 12/13/79 'Herb Alpert: the Rise of a vice-chairman' by Steve Pond

1980's

The New York Times 8/29/84 'Alpert Back at Bandstand –For A Bit by Jon Pareles

The News (MD) 9/24/80 pD-7 'Herb Alpert On his rise with tune' by Yardena Arar
Variety 11/3/82

The Post Standard (NY) pB-47/8/88 'Herb Alpert United Varied Musical Influences' by Carmela Monk

1990's

Billboard 5/l/93 'The A & M in A&M To Exit after 31 Years' by Craig Rosen

New York Times 5/11/95 'Tijuan Brass? Don't Ask" by Donna Perlmutter

San Francisco Chronicle Datebook 4/28/96 p35 'Top Brass' by Aidin Vaziri

2000's

The Herb Alpert File

The Manhattan Mercury 1/5/03 pD1 'getting Sentimental Over Herb' by Mike Dendurent

The New York Times 10/20/05 'Veteran of Tijuana Brass is Back with Midtown Bronze' by James Barron

The Repository 1/6/07 'Alpert, Moss to receive Honor'

Herb Alpert Online:

Please visit these websites for more information on Herb Alpert:

http://www.amcorner.com/forum/

http://www.tijuanabrass.com/

http://www.onamrecords.com/Alpert_Special_Feature.html

http://www.library.ucla.edu/amrecords/index.html
http://www.herbalpert.com/

Herb Alpert Appendixes

About The Author-
Stephen V. O'Rourke is a native of Long Island, New York and has been a lifelong fan of Herb Alpert and his music.
Now living in Singapore, O'Rourke is a graduate of the University of South Australia, (BA Media Management) and the operator of the Internet radio station Singapore365 (live365.com/stations/singapore365)
He can be contacted as stephenvincent62@gmail.com

www.ingramcontent.com/pod-product-compliance
Ingram Content Group UK Ltd.
Pitfield, Milton Keynes, MK11 3LW, UK
UKHW021321180426
11947UKWH00015B/1355

www.ingramcontent.com/pod-product-compliance
Ingram Content Group UK Ltd.
Pitfield, Milton Keynes, MK11 3LW, UK
UKHW021321180426
11947UKWH00015B/1355